What people are saying about ...

MORE OR LESS

"How much is enough? In this important and engaging new book, Jeff makes it clear that when it comes to generosity, connection, and community, too much isn't enough."

Seth Godin, author of *The Icarus Deception*

"Jeff Shinabarger lives this timely message every day. The ideas he gives us in this book are grounded in the credibility of a life that embodies the possibilities."

Gabe Lyons, author of *The Next Christians*

"I genuinely believe that the more you give away, the more you will enjoy what you keep. This book will challenge you to do just that."

Mark Batterson, lead pastor of
National Community Church and
author of *The Circle Maker*

"I am so inspired by this book! With warmth, humility, and brilliant creativity, Jeff Shinabarger challenges us to a journey that can, quite literally, transform our daily lives and those of our neighbors—in our backyard and across the globe. Before I even finished reading the book (which I found hard to put down), I began to notice a shift in my daily thought patterns and decisions, a shift toward more intentionally considering what my family has and what we really need versus what we could give to serve others. Take time to use the tools Jeff has offered for applying this book to your own life, and don't read it alone! Draw your community together and consider what this adventure might hold for you ... and how leveraging your excess with generous abandon might enable the flourishing of others."

Bethany H. Hoang, director of the
IJM Institute for Biblical Justice

"In a society that values abundance, Jeff prompts essential questions that make us aware of what we lose as we gain. Jeff's stories and insights teach us that living a rich life is less about what we own and more about what we do and how we connect with those around us."

Scott Belsky, founder of Behance and
author of *Making Ideas Happen*

"Jeff Shinabarger asks profound questions and shares powerful stories about the relationship between consumerism and community in *More or Less*. The powerful notion of drawing an 'enough line' in our lives has the potential to liberate individuals and unleash a wave of positive impact. *More or Less* is a challenge worth taking."

Doug Shipman, CEO of the National
Center for Civil and Human Rights

"Shifting our imaginations from the pursuit of excess to excessive generosity is life-changing. *More or Less* is a practical guide designed to help us make that shift and experience life to the fullest. Read this book, and you'll never look at life the same way."

Charles Lee, Chief Idea-Maker at Ideation
and author of *Good Idea. Now What?*

"If you're interested in finding the joy of radical generosity and deeper community, this book is for you. This is a madly entertaining book by a leading social activist. Jeff asks a dangerous question—how much is enough?—and highlights stories with the potential to change how we look at wealth and help us rediscover a life of deeper generosity. In his exploration of this question, Jeff not only exposes the danger of excess but also helps us uncover the freedom of simplicity. Read this book and be prepared to be both entertained and challenged to live a fuller life. My friend Jeff is unafraid to ask questions that don't have easy answers. He does so with humor, grace, and wisdom. This book is full of insightful comments that not only bring us to a better understanding of how much is enough but uncover community and generosity in unlikely places."

Peter Greer, president of Hope International
and author of *The Poor Will Be Glad*

"How much is enough? Some books strike a chord with certain people. And other seminal books strike a chord with a certain moment in time. I think Jeff's book captures how we are all thinking right now. It holds up a mirror to our lives, and we may not always like what we see. *More or Less* will challenge you, inspire you, and change you. Now that you can do anything, have everything, and have been everywhere, why does it feel like something is missing? Great books ask great questions. But you will have to supply the answers."

David Hieatt, founder of Do Lectures

"*More or Less* isn't a diatribe about what's wrong; it's a declaration about what works. Jeff shows that when we realize we all have enough, we can help everyone achieve that same level of living and being. He knows that real success doesn't look like getting as much as possible; it's about helping as much as possible. That's an understanding I need to embrace more."

Sam Davidson, cofounder of Cool People
Care and author of *Simplify Your Life*

[+]

MORE

or

LESS

[-]

Choosing a Lifestyle of
Excessive Generosity

JEFF SHINABARGER

David C Cook®
transforming lives together

To Andre.

You live with less, so others have more.

This book was written because I met you.

MORE OR LESS
Published by David C Cook
4050 Lee Vance View
Colorado Springs, CO 80918 U.S.A.

David C Cook Distribution Canada
55 Woodslee Avenue, Paris, Ontario, Canada N3L 3E5

David C Cook U.K., Kingsway Communications
Eastbourne, East Sussex BN23 6NT, England

The graphic circle C logo is a registered trademark of David C Cook.

The website addresses recommended throughout this book are offered as a
resource to you. These websites are not intended in any way to be or imply an
endorsement on the part of David C Cook, nor do we vouch for their content.

Scripture quotations marked NIV are taken from the Holy Bible, New
International Version®, NIV®. Copyright © 1973, 1984 by Biblica, Inc.™ Used
by permission of Zondervan. All rights reserved worldwide. www.zondervan.
com. The author has added italics to Scripture quotations for emphasis.

LCCN 2012955794
ISBN 978-0-7814-0820-2
eISBN 978-1-4347-0555-6

© 2013 Jeff Shinabarger
Published in Association with ChristopherFerebee.com,
Attorney and Literary Agent.

The Team: Alex Field, Amy Konyndyk, Nick Lee, Caitlyn Carlson, Karen Athen
Cover Design: Russell Shaw

Printed in the United States of America
First Edition 2013

1 2 3 4 5 6 7 8 9 10

123112

CONTENTS

FOREWORD /
BOB GOFF

Jeff doesn't just talk about generosity; he lives it. In fact, he and his beautiful wife, Andre, live it like they're made of the stuff. Jeff and Andre have invited me into their lives. Selfishly, I'd like to say I'm one of the very few people who have been invited in because it would make me feel somehow important. But they invite everyone they meet into their lives. Instead of making people feel important, they make everyone feel loved. Where some people act like bouncers when it comes to other people's ideas, Jeff quietly acts like an usher, and in this terrific book he's invited us all to take seats right up front in the orchestra section. He's reminded me once again of what's good in the world and of the simple goodness of giving.

Jeff doesn't set out in this book to convince you that you have much excess stuff in your life—*but he will*. He doesn't try to tell you to let go of the stuff you've accumulated, either—*but you will want to*. What Jeff gently says in this beautifully written book is that we don't just have more stuff than we need; we have more love than we need. In fact, before I turned the last page, I found that I had piles of love hidden everywhere.

Thanks, Jeff, for reminding me where to look.

I've sat with Jeff in the woods in a small cabin where I listened to him talk about big dreams. What is different about Jeff is that his big dreams aren't for him. They are big dreams for other people. And you know what? He makes them happen. You'll see how in this book, and you'll nod your head in agreement like I did—but you won't stop there. You'll go do something about it because love is as contagious as Jeff is.

Among the things I've learned from my time with Jeff in the woods is to be careful who I let into my cabin. Jeff didn't trash the place; instead, he trashed my ideas of creative generosity and how I could go about enacting them. This is the kind of book you'll want to read outside because there will be an explosion of sorts in your life. Some of your ideas of philanthropy will explode. Some of your excuses will explode. Some of your indifference and some of the limits you've put on your love or creativity will explode as well. And if you're like me, you'll find yourself silently mouthing the words "I could do that ..." at the end of many of these chapters. What's even better is that you'll find yourself *doing* those things, not just *thinking* about them any longer. It's for one simple reason—you've found yourself inside the blast radius of Jeff's contagious brand of love.

You'll laugh some and cry some at the stories in this book, but you won't simply agree, because Jeff isn't asking us to just agree with him. Instead, he invites each of us to take the next right step. He doesn't road map the entire journey for us either, but he does offer some pretty good directions.

If love were raindrops, you'd be convinced before you finished this book that Jeff is a tropical storm. I know these things because I've been caught in the squall that surrounds his life, and I've been soaked through with extraordinary love and grace and passion. If you're like me, you'll put down this book and not just want to be more generous; you'll want to be more like Jeff. That's not Jeff's goal of course, but that's what happens when you see love lived out. It's an extravagant love Jeff writes about too. When I got caught in its vortex I found myself wanting to be both at Jeff's side and at the feet of Jesus.

Jeff knows Jesus, and he knows Him well. I don't know this because Jeff told me; I know this because I know Jeff. I've seen him in times of desperate need and in times of utter delight. I've laughed until I've cried as he's told me stories. But none of his stories are about him. They are stories about the needs in the world and the need to help we have in our lives.

Jeff sometimes gets a telltale bird-eating grin on his face, particularly when he's talking about God and how my life would be better if I would shake loose some love. It's almost like Jeff is spinning the dial of the vault in which I keep some of my generosity. In that way, Jeff's not unlike a safecracker listening for tumblers to fall into place. And for me, before I finished the book, they had. Jeff unlocked in me a desire to love God and love people better than I thought I could, with a generosity as creative as it is extravagant.

This is a book of extremes: extreme love, extreme grace, and extreme faith. Jeff is one of those guys all of us hope to have in our lives but few of us do. You're about to meet a guy who will mess with your notions of love and generosity as much as he messed with mine. Let me warn you in advance: your closets, your cabinets, your love, and your pride are not safe around Jeff. That's because Jeff is going to mess with how you use your time, how you spend your money, and what you do with your stuff. Jeff isn't trying to get us to reevaluate our lives; instead he's asked us to value them more. To value what we can give from our excess and what might be possible if we served ourselves up to the world with a large scoop of whimsy.

I'm no meteorologist, but like you, I can smell rain in the wind a long way off, and I could smell this book coming from Jeff for a while. Jeff has given all of us something really beautiful in this book. Jeff hasn't just sprinkled a couple of good ideas in these pages; instead, it's a gully washer of love, creativity, and engagement that a parched world desperately needs. You're about to get caught in the terrific hurricane of kindness that surrounds a guy who loves people well. Buckle up, friends: you are about to get Jeff'ed.

[1]

MORE THAN ENOUGH

An individual has not begun to live until he can rise
above the narrow horizons of his particular individual-
ist concerns to the broader concerns of all humanity.

—*Dr. Martin Luther King Jr.*

Things came to a head the day we moved into East Atlanta Village.

This neighborhood in Atlanta is a quickly developing area of
the city, consisting of a mix of everything from tattoo artists to
college students to African-American leaders who have lived in
the community for fifty years. It has a community-operated bike
shop and eclectic bars featuring the best up-and-coming young
musicians, and the contrast of brand-new craftsman-style homes
and homes that were hand-painted in the 1950s. It's a wonderful,
diverse place to live.

My wife and I, as we considered moving into the city of
Atlanta, loved the vibe of being in the village. We also liked the
idea that we would live close to great places to eat and hang out.

We stepped up from a two-bedroom to a three-bedroom home with a great yard for our dog, Max. We knew this was going to be the place where we started a family. We believed that this would be the place where our lives would progress in ways we had not experienced previously.

We just didn't expect what would happen next.

Some neighborhoods have welcoming committees. Others have the unofficial but genetically friendly neighbor who brings over cookies or a bottle of wine when she notices someone moving into the vacant house on the street. When we moved into our house, it was only a few hours before a man rang the doorbell.

This was our neighborhood welcoming committee of one.

He had one of those smiles that implied he had some hard stories to tell. His teeth were a little crooked, yet very white. He wore a Cincinnati Reds hat sitting cocked to one side. He was about forty-five years old and not afraid to talk to anyone. I quickly learned to recognize the particular way he rang the doorbell: much longer than the average person. My new neighbor's name was Clarence, and as I learned that day, he was always "looking for work." I also learned that Clarence worked hard. He focused on one project at a time much better than I ever could. He was a proud worker and enjoyed telling us about all the ways he made our neighborhood a better place, specifically by painting the neighbor's house by himself. You can't miss it: an electric blue house at the corner of my street. That house seems a perfect representation of Clarence: exposed and visible for all to see, because Clarence had no home.

Clarence belonged to a sociological category taught about in the issues-focused classes offered at my liberal-arts college. Clarence was one of the hundreds and thousands counted and written about in statistical articles I had read in newspapers, magazines, and online numerous times. Discussing ethics and studying statistics may spark an intellectual motivation to do the right thing, but meeting a person who was my literal neighbor took doing the right thing to a new level. It's not that I'd never met a homeless person before. I'd served in soup kitchens, fixed up overnight shelters, the usual right things to do. But this was different. Clarence pushed me over the edge. He was my neighbor. I couldn't get away from him. And I liked him. His constant smirk of a smile got under my skin and into my heart.

I enjoyed a complicated friendship with Clarence from the beginning. Our relationship introduced a barrage of new questions for my life: *how do I love my neighbor when my neighbor has no front door or even walls?* My previous worldview assumed my neighbor would live in the same context as me: in a home. I thought the fabric on our couch or our dinner choices might be different, but I never really imagined my neighbor without a refrigerator or a shower. Loving your neighbor is a great virtue in life, but this neighbor brought new complications to mine.

With one doorbell ring, all the ways I looked at my day-to-day life changed. Suddenly I began to see my life through Clarence's eyes. What he saw looking through my front door was abundance. I have not one but two living areas that anyone can actually see from the front door. If I lived in New Orleans they would refer to my home as a shotgun house—a straight hallway from the front door to the back. I have air-conditioning for those hot days in Atlanta. I have a toilet and shower in each of my two bathrooms, and I even have a washer and dryer for my clothes. And speaking of clothes, my wife and I each have our own walk-in closet filled with them. I have a shed, and my shed is full of tools. My shed holds a bike that I can choose to ride if it is a nice day, and a lawn mower with an extra gallon of gas, just in case. I easily have more than enough. Clarence didn't have to say a thing to me. Just having this new relationship in my life changed the way that I looked at the world.

My material excess and his material need made for a confusing symbiotic relationship. At the start, our relationship felt oppressively lopsided, as it was entirely dependent upon whether I granted his regular requests for money, work, or food. I decided to feed him or give him money for the work he did in our yard. It was always my decision. This raised a number of questions for me: *is this how a relationship should be? Is it really all about me and what Clarence can do for me? What can I learn from him? What would I gain by knowing him?* I didn't really have the answers, but I didn't give up. He kept ringing my doorbell, and I kept opening the door.

After many months of intense conversations on our front porch, during which I learned more about Clarence while laughing together and working together, I realized that our relationship had transitioned. Once he asked to use my phone, so I showed him my iPhone. "Your i-what?" he responded. He didn't know how to use it, but after a quick lesson and placing his call, he told me I needed to get a real phone because the sound was too quiet.

As he left a voicemail, I overheard him say, "Now you have my number. Just call me back, and my friend Jeff will find me." It was a strange moment for me as I realized that in that moment I became both his personal assistant and his friend.

Somehow we reached a new level of dignity in our relationship. He found in me a sense of community, as if I had a small glimpse of understanding into the life that he lived. We both knew there was no way that I could fully grasp what it would feel like not to have a physical place to sit down and process the day. But there was also an understanding that he could never fully understand the things that I have been given. Our worlds were far apart, yet we lived in the same square mile. We became friends, and our individual lives transitioned to a deeper collaboration and understanding.

Most of the things I learned from Clarence grew out of the extreme frustration rooted in our extreme differences. He didn't see the world the same way I did, and it was tough. The selfish way that I see the world was always called into question when I was with Clarence. Every time I heard his long doorbell ring, it was like an alarm sounding his need. Without Clarence I wouldn't think about how people on the street feel when it rains. Without Clarence I wouldn't know that not all homeless people are looking for handouts. Without Clarence I wouldn't think about how the changing seasons and temperatures influence the living conditions of the impoverished. Without Clarence I wouldn't understand what it means to love my neighbor. Without Clarence I wouldn't understand that I have more than enough.

I wish everyone had the opportunity to know someone like Clarence. When we become friends with people who have more or less than we do, like Clarence, it causes us to live differently.

It causes us to see more. It causes us to think about living with less.

At one level, this book is a way for me to share my journey of learning from people like Clarence and to introduce other friends walking a similar path. On this path, we've encountered people and places and situations that stop us in our tracks and cause us to rethink the way we live our lives. We've met people we have begun to love, places that desperately need the light of hope, and situations that beg for solutions. This journey forced us to make distinct and necessary changes in our own lives. Every story that you read is one that has caused me to change. I hope these stories do the same for you. Together we will ask questions, make hypotheses, and embark on some new experiments.

This is my story of change.

The reason I am writing is to share my experiences with you. To share with you a new understanding of what is enough in this life. I have more than enough, and I believe many people, possibly even you, have more than enough as well. Questions are the root of everything great I have done in life. The most creative ideas ever experienced are often conceptualized by asking simple questions. So that is where we need to start this journey: with a question.

I invite you to join me in a series of social experiments that challenge us to ask *what is enough?* in life. This question may begin to challenge the way you see the world today. That's okay. When we choose to draw a line in every aspect of our lives, we choose what is enough. We are given the opportunity to define what is enough. There is great tension in walking this line of more or less, but this tension creates great opportunities. Living on less creates the potential to do much more for others.

May we be known by the problems we solve.

It all starts with one question that changes everything: *what is enough?*

● *Visual Moment*
Watch the full story of Jeff and Clarence:
www.moreorlessbook.com/#videos

[2]

ONE MAN'S JUNK

Character cannot be developed in ease and quiet.
Only through experience of trial and suffering
can the soul be strengthened, vision cleared,
ambition inspired, and success achieved.

—*Helen Keller*

When Andre and I got engaged and started preparing for marriage, our community was extremely excited and encouraging. For some reason, all our married friends wanted to get together and have a meal with us. We soon understood that what they really wanted was to sit us down and give marriage advice. If you're reading this and are one of the couples that we had dinner with before we were married, thanks for the advice (it's been ten incredible years). There is always something special about sitting around a table and eating food together. Having a meal with friends physically fills you up, emotionally encourages your passions, spiritually lifts your soul, and naturally fuels the desire for laughter.

Coming straight out of college, a good meal and some valuable advice was a great engagement gift! But with all these wonderful opportunities for connection and advice, the extremely practical (and maybe opportunistic) part of me wondered what else we might gain from these great connections. I know that sounds like a very selfish statement, and it is. We had a dilemma: in just a couple of months we would be moving from our college dorm rooms to an apartment in Chicago, and we had nothing to move. We owned no furniture. So I came up with an idea to solve this problem.

Here's my theory: I believe all Americans with homes have a piece of furniture that they hate; all they need is for someone to take it away, and they will freely offer it up. My theory goes a step further: I believe that the family will cheer you on as you carry it away, as if a battle has finally been won among them and that ugly end table. They are dying for someone to take it off their hands. Every family has something in their home that they do not want, but for some reason it's still sitting in the living room or taking up space in the basement. Is my theory correct?

The beginnings of this theory started in high school. Once, we played this neighborhood scavenger hunt game with some friends—perhaps you've heard of it? Each team starts with a tooth-pick and a time frame for how long the game will last—usually about two hours. We went door to door through our neighbor-hood, hoping complete strangers would actually open the door. Then we asked them if they would like to make a "trade up." Would they give us something in their home for something that was in our hands? The winner at the end of the game is the person with the biggest and best thing. It's all, as they say, in "the power of the ask," which also happens to be one of my favorite phrases. The worst someone could do was say no. We asked them, "What would you trade us for a toothpick?" And it surprised us all how quickly the game progressed toward much larger items.

Let's play the game out to give you a glimpse of the progression. A toothpick might turn into a can of soup or a box of macaroni and cheese. It quickly escalates to a candle or an old beach towel. Maybe you get lucky and get an obscure painting from someone's basement or a necklace that someone doesn't like anymore. By the end of the two hours, friends run back to the starting location with the most surprised faces as they carry back a couch, a bag of golf clubs, a Ping-Pong table, or a lawn mower. There is a convergence of groups running down the street, trying to carry some big things together while dodging oncoming cars and barking dogs. One time when we played, a team returned with one of those mosquito zappers that emits a radiant blue haze of light. Where do you even buy one of those?[1]

Years later, I heard this game played over the radio in Atlanta when the morning team of The Bert Show on Q100 played it with hundreds and thousands of morning listeners. They called the game "Tradio." They wanted to see if they could get a physical house by the end of the game. People would call in and trade up accordingly.[2] By the time I had signed off, they had acquired both a hot tub and a horse. It is truly amazing to see what you can accumulate in such a short time. Once again, it seems that most of us have much more stuff than we actually use, need, or want. We seem to always be looking for a way to "trade up" from what we have, to get something better. Bigger. Faster. Stronger. *We want more.*

So back to our engagement—Andre and I would go to dinner after dinner, and at the end of the conversation our friends and mentors would ask us, "Is there anything that we can do for you? Just let us know." Most people wouldn't dream of actually *asking* for something, given the reality that dinner was already a gift—but not me. Remember my favorite phrase, "the power of the ask"? I would look at Andre, and she would glare at me, full of dread, and roll her eyes.

"Well, we have just graduated from college and don't have a thing for our new apartment," I began. "There is a theory that I have … Do you have any furniture in your home that you are trying to get rid of? Well, we don't have anything for our new apartment, so we would love to take it off your hands."

As you can imagine, Andre's face would go beet red, and she would start to sink farther down into her seat.

Though it was embarrassing, my theory worked. By the time we moved into our apartment, we had two couches, three side tables, a brand-new queen bed with the head and foot boards, a washer and dryer, a couple of lamps, and a bookshelf.

I think I was told no only once.

Most people thought my theory was true. It became a great laugh over and over again. The couple sitting with us would instantly nod their heads, thinking of the exact piece of furniture they needed to get rid of from their home. And for the record, we still have that bookshelf in our living room and sleep in our free bed.

I HAVE EXCESS

What this little theory taught me was that many people have excess. Excess is that thing that we could give away today, and it wouldn't change a single aspect of our tomorrow. Excess is more than what we need—and in turn it may be exactly what someone else needs. Anything more than enough is excess. Excess is margin. Excess is more than enough.

We have an uncanny ability to accumulate things that are not essential to living, yet we lack the practice of releasing the acquired junk when it no longer serves a purpose. I am no different. I have gone from begging furniture off my friends to having a houseful of things I could give to a newly engaged couple trying to fill an apartment. While I may struggle to define what *is* enough for me, one thing is sure:

I have more than enough.

I have more than I need in numerous categories: food, clothing, shelter, toys, books, blankets, TV channels, and maybe even friends.

I WANT MORE

When John D. Rockefeller was asked, "What is enough?" Rockefeller's reply was, "Just a little bit more."

Rockefeller was one of the wealthiest men in history. So why would he say this? While I can't relate to Rockefeller's wealth,

I can relate to Rockefeller's desire. He had exponentially more zeros in his bank account than the rest of us could ever dream of having. Yet our struggle is the same. He wanted more, and I want more. My desires don't end easily. I can't keep up with others. Others have the new technological gadget that is solving all of life's problems, or a big enough car that fits everything they need for a long road trip. They have a cleaning service, HBO, or a pool. Others have more friends on Facebook, season tickets, or that cool boat for weekend excursions. They have more goodies than me. They have stuff that I want. They have more. Bill McKibben, in his book *Deep Economy*,[3] taught me that while we desire more, we instinctively know that more is not always better. Something deep inside us knows that money and even the stuff that money buys does not guarantee happiness, yet I still want just a little more.

What is enough, and what is excess?

Where do I draw a line?

How do I draw a line?

When it comes to drawing lines, I have come to the stark realization that I probably will not sell my possessions and run the streets naked like St. Francis of Assisi did all those years ago. I won't leave my family and join a religious society, donating all I have to nurse the dying, like Mother Theresa did. I probably won't make a radical change in my appearance and start sewing my own clothes like Shane Claiborne and the Simple Way[4] in Philadelphia. As much as I respect these great leaders' stories as radical and admirable, I am not them. I am me.

I enjoy technological advancements. I get excited to try out a new restaurant. I don't live as simply as some. My life is unusually advantaged compared to the world and especially compared to my neighbor Clarence. I would assume that many reading this book can probably relate more to me than to Assisi or Claiborne. Chances are, you have more than enough, like I do. We acquired enough education that we are literate and value reading as a way to continue our education even without outside requirements. Not only do we know how to read, we earn enough expendable income to buy this book. We possess enough free time to sit quietly and read the book in a comfortable chair with a fluffy pillow to one side of our back. Our chair is probably sitting in a room that is climate-controlled in some way. This room is in a building with a roof, floor, and walls, and most likely this room has multiple smoke detectors to alert us of potential danger. This building is surrounded by a manicured yard with some form of transportation sitting steps away from the front door to take us wherever we want to go, whenever we want to go there. Given these simple categories, you and I probably have more in common than we might have otherwise realized. We probably have more than we need.

Enough already.

Many of us don't want our stories to end with just an understanding that we have been given much. We want to do more with what we have; we just don't know how to combat a culture that defines so much of what we think we need. In contrast to the American idea of increasing the monetary assets in our lives, I believe we also desire to increase our portfolio of generosity. Giving to the needs of people always results in a greater equation of life worth.

More than ever, people want to give. We want to give to others that are in great need, but too often we are paralyzed by our own possessions that cripple our ability to begin our journey toward generosity. Our excess has taken away eyes to see where there is need and how we can help. We have become blind toward need, resulting in our hands and feet becoming paralyzed toward the actionable pursuit of giving.

I NEED TO SEE NEED

One of the reasons we fail to see the connections between what we have and what others need is simple geography. Our communities and culture have sheltered our lives away from direct contact with the needs of others. For example, in our own homes we have designed our lives away from community. We build fences around our backyards to separate ourselves from our neighbors. We park our cars in garages, which allows us to individually walk directly into our homes without any interaction with people on our street. We even set up passwords on our wireless networks to limit outside use of our Internet access.

On an even larger scale, developers build cities and design streets to direct drivers toward desirable places that increase the local economy and shelter people from lower-income locations. This is a historical truth to the design in my city, Atlanta, where leaders implemented a street-sweeping initiative prior to the 1996 Olympics to sweep away any signs of homelessness. This measure translated into simply arrest-ing the homeless to make the city appear clean and shiny to tourists and the cameras of the Olympic coverage. This is a very common strategy in cities trying to portray an image to the global camera.

These strategies focus on what others see looking in from the outside and are aimed at developing the economy, which is a good thing for the perception of the city and job creation. But these strate-gies also result in separating the affluent from the hurts and struggles that exist in all our communities. Unfortunately, the strategies that separate us from the suffering in our communities also create cal-loused hearts closed to issues of injustice, lacking empathy. Needs still exist but are masked or not seen by walls of segmentation.

When Clarence rang my doorbell that first day, he touched a button into my soul that had not previously been revealed. Suddenly right on my front porch I saw my neighbor and his need in stark contrast to my life and excess. In retrospect, that was exactly what *I* needed. I believe we can all take a lesson from Clarence and create some bridges by walking across some streets to meet our neighbors, both literally and figuratively. And as we see the needs of others up close, we may see exactly where our excess can be best used to help someone else.

A GENERATION OF GENEROSITY

I believe that deep down we are all generous people, but that most of us just do not get the opportunity to see where our generosity can help others. We need to see opportunities of great need to engage in generosity.

I experienced this personally in 2005. It started with a nightmare. I dreamed of a boy about eight years old, four feet tall, no shirt—only ripped up, mud-stained pants—with a big little belly. I still can't remember what his face looked like. It was like a Hype Williams music video where he focuses on the sun gleaming around the product he wants you to see. In my dream, suddenly the angle of the sun moved, and an empty glass appeared. The boy leaned down to fill the glass with water again, and the shot panned back in a cinematic style. I watched the boy dip the glass into a filthy puddle on a mud street. He took another drink. I woke up.

It was 3:27 in the morning. I was sweating. I went to the kitchen, filled up a glass of ice water from my refrigerator door, and took a drink. I woke Andre up. She told me I needed to do something about the dream. It seemed ridiculous to do something instantly after a dream, but sometimes radical ideas need people to make them come to life.

That nightmare birthed in me a responsibility to educate others on the need for clean water and how easy it was to solve this problem. I shared the idea with my good friend Gabe Lyons, who gave it legs. We decided to launch the idea of bringing clean water to Rwanda at an event called Catalyst that I have led creatively for eight years. Catalyst gathers thousands of young leaders together every year, and it creates a platform to make significant cultural change across the nation. We asked a question: what would happen if we educated this community and gave them an opportunity to respond? We did this in 2005, before clean water became a sexy cause. Very few people knew of the need. As they entered Catalyst the first morning, every person was given a bottle of water: no explanation, no tag, no branding, no cost—just pure clean water. Then we shared the story of the need. We take clean water for granted in America. The reality is that if there were clean water in developing countries today, sickness and illnesses would be cut literally in half. The leaders responded by giving $134,000 in ten minutes—a drop in the bucket.

In the spring of 2006, a group of fifteen of us went to Rwanda to report on the first wells that had been dug since that ten-minute offering. That was one of the proudest and most humbling moments of my life. We saw how the simplest modern convenience changed the health and hope of an entire village. It was such a simple solution, yet it changed a village forever. I learned very quickly that a small offering has the ability to change a society.

We came home and were humbled by how many lives were changed and how little we did to make such a substantial difference for thousands of people in Rwanda. The money kept coming in the mail. It was beyond anything I could have ever dreamed. Thirty kids made beautiful artwork on ceramic pitchers they sold on eBay. A church in Alabama had a free-will offering on a Sunday morning that totaled seventy thousand dollars. A coffee shop in Orlando found a matching donor for a fund-raiser at their business and raised twelve thousand dollars. Three years later, we had raised nearly two million dollars toward clean water in Rwanda.

Through this project, I learned that this generation cares about others. When someone is suffering, we want to be the people to end injustice. When others are hurting, we want to help. Our generation is generous; we want to give. If our generation gets the opportunity to see the need, we want to change the situation and join in offering redemption to the brokenness.

OUR EXCESS CAN ADDRESS NEEDS

A street sweep took on a whole new meaning for me the first time I visited the Kibera Slums in Nairobi, Kenya. I am no expert on the complexities of Kibera. It's difficult to nail down how many people live in this small space, but many people explain it as roughly one million people living within one square mile. It's located directly next to downtown Nairobi, right in the heart of the city, and you will find small shack upon shack upon shack that these loving people call their homes. These homes are mostly made of tin and sit under the biggest high-rises in the nation. It's a great juxtaposition of buildings. The contrasting structures are a memorable image to anyone who has experienced it. My wife, Andre, worked at Kibera for a summer with a clinic, serving critical medical needs and giving vaccinations and much-needed treatments to victims of HIV. She introduced me to this neighborhood. Many Non-Governmental Organizations (NGOs) do amazing work to serve the needs of Kibera, but the solutions are complex, and it continues to be a place of great need and confusion. And one conversation I had on that trip forever changed how I saw the world.

When I first arrived and walked around the city, my initial thought was that someone simply needed to clean the streets and introduce a new standard of living—at least in an environmental context—just like Mayor Rudy Giuliani changed the streets of New York by refusing to let vandalism and trash define the city.[5] Granted, the success of this philosophy is debated continuously. But I saw a need and felt compelled to look for a solution. Andre quickly dismissed my suggestion with a statement that changed the way I look at both trash and the complexity of Kibera.

She said, "These people rely on the trash for economy. These creative friends of mine make things out of what we call trash and sell the products for income. If we take away the trash, we are taking away their dignity and opportunity. This trash is a lifeline and hope in the midst of suffering. What we see as trash, they see as an essential material that may end their hunger. The trash creates something to make. The trash creates jobs. The trash provides money. The trash is their canvas for art."

I didn't suggest another solution the rest of my time at Kibera. My simplified solutions were so elementary compared to the compounding challenges that exist. As you can see, I was an uneducated person as it relates to the suffering of these people. I had never experienced this place before, but my eyes were opened. Andre had relationships with real people in this important place. She'd been using her "excess"—her knowledge of basic medical care—to serve those in need. By spending time in Kibera and making friends, she developed a deep respect for the people and their suffering. She set the example for me to stop offering quick answers and choose instead to listen to the people in the community. Though I felt overwhelmed by layer upon layer of challenges that her friends faced, my admiration for them grew every day.

Have you ever considered that *one person's trash may create hope and opportunity for another person?*

Social entrepreneurs all over the world are creating a better environment by cleaning up what is excess and turning it into new creations, and in some of the developing countries this innovation is leading our world. We experienced the story of trash to beauty as we went house to house in the trading-up game, and we felt it personally when friends gave us furniture during our engagement. But in Kibera, for the first time we met people who relied on trash for their livelihood. Our excess can make a difference, but we first have to see need in our society and opportunity for all people. When we see need, we are also introduced to opportunity—opportunity to understand our excess more fully.

ONE QUESTION CHANGES EVERYTHING

The sad truth is that while others fight for survival, we all want a little bit more. When we get more we tend to spend more, which results in wanting more. Meanwhile, we throw away what others need for survival. It's a disturbing circle of want and need, but we have the ability to change the cycle. The change begins when we acknowledge that our excess creates an opportunity to address the needs of others.

What is enough?

This may be the most critical question of our generation. More important, it may be the most critical question of our personal lives. If we do not make a personal choice to draw a line, we will be taken over by desire. Defining enough is our personal responsibility. We won't recognize *enough* in our lives unless we have taken the time to define that line. Defining *enough* leads to a freedom in life that is just waiting to be experienced, breaking the bondage of our ever-increasing desires. I've just begun to experience this freedom. As I have put the question to various aspects of my life, I am finding that asking the question does not limit me as much as it grants me sanity. When I define enough, I step off the conveyor belt of consumerism and create my own rhythm of life. Over time, advertisers, credit cards, and the quest for more and better lose their control over me. I no longer feel pushed around by others telling me what I need and want. Enough is a realistic measuring stick—one that offers me attainable and sustainable goals for life and the pursuit of my calling. Sometimes less can do more.

If you look up *enough* in the dictionary, you will find a subjective definition: "Adequate for the want or need; sufficient for the purpose or to satisfy desire."[6]

Want or need? Sufficiency or satisfaction? Purpose or desire? The gulf between these words is impossible to measure, and therefore the breadth of this definition is endless. This is a definition that leaves space for anything.

The definition of *enough* cannot be defined by or for others. It would be much easier if someone gave each of us a definition to live by, but it isn't that easy. *Enough* isn't a percentage of your income. There is no simple formula. Every person must define what is enough individually. I can't determine for you what you need more of and where you could choose less. As I continue to define what enough looks like for me, I have found that it is much easier to critique someone else's definition and lifestyle. I don't recommend it. Not only will it cause others to avoid you and your potentially judgmental observations, it also doesn't do you any good. It's hard enough to process your own motivations, needs, and desires without trying to evaluate everyone else's. Work on your own personal definition of enough.

One tangible way you can keep the focus on yourself is to keep a piece of paper in this book as you read. As you finish each chapter, sketch a line with a plus sign (more than enough) on one end of the paper and a minus sign (less than enough) on the other. Ask yourself, *where am I on this spectrum for this specific topic? Do I need more or do I want more? When will I have enough?* Some topics may bring great conflict to your life, while in other areas you will be content. The important thing is to draw your line of enough.

Always remember that others can speak into this process, but only you can define where you draw the line. Think through where you are on the line—needing more, having excess, or possessing just enough. Then consider what you might need to change. In which direction would you like to move? Keep the focus on evaluating yourself and what you feel prompted to do, give, or try. And don't be afraid to take action toward enough. Walk that line on a daily basis. I believe anything we find that is more than enough creates an immediate opportunity to make others' lives better.

WE WILL BE KNOWN BY THE
PROBLEMS WE SOLVE

Answering the question in every aspect of life can define who you are, how others see you, and what legacy you will leave for humanity. In our society, the question is not whether we have excess, but rather what we will do with our excess. How will we turn our excess into action? What if individuals chose to live in contrast to the American dream and chose a story line different from the normal white-picket-fence picture? A dream should be a personal pursuit of passion and adventure because no one wants to live in the standardized world of *The Truman Show*. We all need to find our own space, our own dream, and our own gift to give.

As I began to form my own rough outline of enough and pursue my unique dream, I met others feeling the same calling. My friends and I put our creative minds together to explore creative ways to use our excess for good. I like to call them social experiments. We designed these experiments to challenge our current lifestyles and to cast light on our excess. From counting clothes to recovering change on leftover gift cards, we began asking the question: what if we created a culture that asked, "What is enough?" Maybe we could exchange our lives of excess for a collaborative community pursuing generosity. Maybe we could find purpose behind why we have been given so much.

Our goal from the beginning was not to feel guilt but rather to feel grateful for our excess and then begin to bless friends around us out of our abundance. We don't believe personal wealth is wrong; rather, it is an opportunity that we hope will result in a lifestyle of greater generosity. This generous lifestyle will bring joy and freedom in a society dedicated to the pursuit of gaining more for *me*. Maybe this is our chance to create a societal shift from feeding unnecessary desires to addressing issues of suffering throughout the world.

We invite you to join us.

TWO BAGS OF TRASH

I had talked about doing it for a few weeks. Finally, I got off the couch and moved. I opened the door of the kitchen cabinet under the sink and took out two big black trash bags. I walked out through our front door, down the driveway, and began.

For weeks I had noticed trash on the streets and sidewalks of our neighborhood, and unlike in Kibera, no one was using this trash for anything good. So I started. There was nothing glamorous about the work, but I reminded myself that sometimes it is important to work for your community even when it doesn't feel like you are doing much. I leaned over, and with just two fingers I gingerly picked up a cup and straw from a fine fast-food establishment called Checkers down the street. I tried not to think about what germs might be multiplying on this nasty cup and made a mental note to buy a pair of gloves for next time. I moved on down the street and picked up pieces from a broken pot on the sidewalk. I picked up candy-bar wrappers. A few liquor bottles.

Beer cans. Coke bottles. Empty bags of chips. Glass fragments. A plastic bag. A syringe. (*Oh, God, protect me!*) Gum wrappers. On and on. It didn't stop. One bag was full. Then I picked up a bag from McDonalds. More cups. More wrappers. More trash.

Then it happened. A homeless guy I had never seen in my life yelled at me from across the street. "Hey, I think you missed a few," he shouted. "Over there in the bushes, you missed a few." *Thanks (I think …)*, I thought.

I picked up the trash in the bushes and realized my two bags were full, so I turned around and started walking home. As I walked back just four blocks, I saw more and more trash littering the streets and parking lots that I hadn't even touched and didn't have enough space for in my two measly trash bags. I put the trash in our green trash bin and walked back in the front door. Done, but not done at all.

As I slumped down on the couch, trying to feel good about what I had done, I realized what I'd just experienced. It was a short story of what we all hope to do and what we all have to overcome and what we all hate to do and what we all need to do and what it takes to leave an imprint on this world.

We live in a world with so many problems. Media inundates us with image after image of overwhelming need. We want to make the world better. We want to change how we see the world. Sometimes just getting started is the biggest hurdle. Then we finally dive in and realize that dealing with messes means we might get dirty. We actually have to touch the problem. Let me warn you now: there are plenty of chances to quit along the way to making a difference. But we can choose to sweat it out, tackle our feelings of discomfort, and work through the messiness of the problem. Just as we begin to feel good and truly invest, working to figure out how to get a win in solving the problem, a guy with no vested interest, no sweat equity, no voice that has a right to be heard, yells from the stands and tries to bring us down. It's the last thing we need to hear in that moment, but for some reason we listen. We question everything we do. *Can we really even make a dent in this problem?* The problem is so big, and we are so small. *Are we even making a difference?* We start to analyze everything we do, but we courageously push through and finish the day.

We go home and hope for new energy to keep going.

We go to sleep.

We wake up the next morning.

And we do it again. Why? Because if we don't do it, not a single other person in the world feels the same responsibility to make it right. I believe there is a problem in this world that you were called to solve. It is your responsibility to find that problem and make it right. It's not the way it ought to be, and it can be better. This problem matters. It may not matter to anyone else on earth, but it matters to me. It matters to you. It is the start to a new way of living. We will mark this day as the beginning of something significant.

You and I have an opportunity. We are tomorrow, and the future rides on our shoulders. We see brokenness, and we want to make a difference. We stand with two hands open. On the one hand we are hopeful, and on the other hand fear fills us. Fear of what we will be forced to change within ourselves. Our passion to bring good pushes our dreams forward. We believe we can make the world a better place. We may only influence a few, or we may change the course of history. Either way, it's worth it. We must overcome our apathy.

Perhaps this simplistic and poetic view of life seems unreasonable and different. And we probably feel that way *because it is.* We know others can't understand the vision growing within us, and the ideas in our minds are much loftier than may seem possible. Our mission is to create something that will end suffering for one other person. That person is worth everything. It is time to change because this hope is too big not to pursue. Nothing will hold us back. We have enough, and we will give more. It starts by wrestling with two words: *more* and *less.*

ENOUGH TALK

In every chapter, I hope to engage you with something to do, an actionable project. You will read stories of leaders who created a new definition of enough. I hope to offer various angles on this concept so you can engage this question within your own life and family. At the end of each chapter, I will give you something to do to take your reading into real life, to stop thinking or talking and start doing.

Here is where you start on that journey.

For the next week, every day, listen to the words of your friends or colleagues. Try to hear what others communicate as a need or want. Your goal is to begin to give to others out of things that you already have in your possession. They may just need to borrow something, or you may choose to give them a gift with no strings attached. Listen to statements like this: "I really need _____." "I could really use a _____." "I have been wanting to get _____."

Try to think about everyday things in your home that you could give to make a friend's life easier and your life simpler. Match something you have in your possession with a need of a friend. No strings attached. Just let it go. Give it away. Be generous. Give something larger than usual. You will be amazed how others will respond positively and with surprise. Get a taste of what it feels like to give out of your excess this week.

THE KITCHEN PANTRY

In Africa there is a concept known as *ubuntu*—the
profound sense that we are human only through the
humanity of others; that if we are to accomplish
anything in this world it will in equal measure be
due to the work and achievement of others.

—*Nelson Mandela*

I knew that this new concept of determining what is enough could not happen unless I chose to live out this question and wrestle with the answers. The reality hit me particularly hard one January day when I received our credit-card bill in the mail. This was the infamous, dreaded after-Christmas credit-card bill. It seemed that we spent a bit more that Christmas than we intended, and we owed about $1,600 on our credit card from Christmas gifts alone. It was one of those situations where my love language of gift-giving bit us in the butt. We did not have $1,600 to pay the bill. This forced us to cut back in some areas of our budget and make some difficult decisions to be able to pay the bills. First off, we decided not to buy clothes for the next two months. That was an easy solution, since we received some new clothes for Christmas. We decided not to buy anything special for the house or for the yard. No movies. And still, we were short on cash. I had a (self-proclaimed) brilliant idea. What if we didn't buy any groceries for the entire month?

"Are you crazy?" Andre replied.

"No, really, I think that we can live for the next month on all the food in our kitchen pantry, refrigerator, and freezer," I said.

"What about milk?"

"We can go buy a gallon of milk if that is an essential."

"Okay. Let's do it. No-grocery January. And I will go buy some milk."

My always-adventurous wife was all in.

And so it began. Our first intentional, organized social experiment:

What is enough food?

We started with the meats in the freezer, and when mixed with a bag of rice and steamed veggies, we felt proud of our healthy meal. *This is doable*, we thought. After three days we ran out of all the fresh vegetables & fruits. We started digging deeper ... we had three boxes of corn muffins we worked through with some chili. Deeper. We found five freezer-burned Lean Cuisine dinners in the bottom of the freezer. Deeper. The two boxes of brownies and the cake mix were a highlight for me. We got to the bottom of the freezer and found a package of six frozen unbaked loaves of bread. Score. We baked all of them. One loaf would last a few days, then we'd put another in the oven. We ran out of butter for the bread and eventually worked through all our olive oil. We ate canned soup. More canned soup. Spaghetti. Noodles with no sauce. The last box of macaroni and cheese. Canned tuna. At some point in the process, I realized I had not actually ever seen the back of the cupboard before that moment. We found some small bottles of Mott's apple juice. More canned soup. JELL-O. And Ramen Noodles, they never go bad, right? Oh, and we had about twenty little packets of Kool-Aid. Lastly, we made pancakes … three times.

We committed to going a month without grocery shopping. At the end, we lasted seven weeks without going to the grocery store once. Also, I think I gained about seven pounds from all the starches and carbohydrates we ate. I wouldn't recommend eating this way, but this small experiment helped us to evaluate the food excess we already owned without realizing it. And this simple, actionable social experiment launched this journey to define what is enough for our lives.

We had nearly two months of groceries sitting in our kitchen pantry and didn't even know it. We didn't realize how much food we had tucked away in our cupboards. How did we get to this place? Storage. We realized this principle: the more space we create for storage, the more we fill up that space with stuff. As our kitchen got larger, our need to fill it grew as well. This resulted in more kitchen appliances, dishes, and food in the larger pantry. We all want more storage because we feel like we need to organize our things to simplify our belongings, but we don't always consider the implications of how that contributes to our own excess. As we organize our stuff with labels and bins, we find easier ways to tuck away more things. Being more organized does not mean we are living any simpler; it only means we are living more organized. In actuality, when we are organized, it's easier to hold onto more stuff because everything has order and a place. With every additional square foot we add to our lives, we claim dominion and multiply our possessions by filling that space with stuff.

When we were newly married, Andre and I rented a six-hundred-square-foot apartment in Chicago (filled with all that free furniture we rescued from friends). It was a tiny space. We had one door in the entire apartment, and it led to the bathroom. I remember that bathroom very clearly. Whenever we got into an argument that first year of marriage, one of us would lock ourselves in the bathroom; it was the only place to get away. The only room with a door. At the time we thought it was horrible, but in hindsight, it wasn't so bad. Our kitchen was four feet by seven feet at most and it included a refrigerator, stove, oven, and sink. We had a total of two square feet of counter space in the entire kitchen, which was just big enough to dry dishes. We did the dishes after every meal because if we didn't we wouldn't have any counter space for our toaster. It was very small. But it was enough.

For some reason, after the groceries experiment I wanted to go back to that apartment. I miss those days. Life was much simpler. We bought groceries once per week because we couldn't fit any more into the space. As a result, the food we bought was usually fresh and healthy. We walked down the street to the farmer's market and bought fresh produce every Saturday. We didn't have to worry about the date the groceries might go bad because they never had the opportunity. There was no space for going bad. There was no space for more of anything. So what did we do? We got a bigger place. And a bigger place. And a bigger place. Until one day we did a social experiment and skipped buying groceries for seven weeks.

There is an ironic daily occurrence that happens around 6:00 p.m. in homes all over the country. Someone opens the refrigerator, gazes for approximately twenty seconds, and calls out, "Hey, honey, there's nothing to eat in the house!"

Why do we say that? Why would we think that? There *is* something to eat in our homes. In my house there were actually 147 meals in the house (three meals a day for seven weeks). For some reason, our rational minds have lost touch with reality when it relates to this topic.

To think that most of the world can't eat one meal today while I could eat 147 meals just on the food sitting in my kitchen—how can this be? Why would I have this much food stored up in excess on my shelves? I must be a little indulgent. I hope I am the only person facing this reality, but I have a feeling that I'm not alone.

How many weeks could you and your family last living off of the food sitting in your kitchen right now?

Bobby Bailey has a different angle on asking, "What is enough food?" He is a creative leader in the world of humanitarian awareness and justice relief work, most notably known for being one of the three guys who told the story of Invisible Children.[1] He broke off from his partners to continue to bring creative expressions to meet needs in the world. He brought a radical new campaign to the United States in an effort called Live Below The Line.[2] Live Below the Line was educated by The World Bank, which sets the "extreme poverty" standard ($1.25 per day). This standard forms the "extreme poverty line," a mark that is shared by 1.4 billion people.[3] In zeros, that number looks like this: 1,400,000,000. Something about all those zeros makes my heart skip a beat. After seeing up close just a few of those people who are suffering, Bobby Bailey felt compelled to be a part of the solution.

Live Below The Line is a challenge to go five days living on only $1.25 per day. As the organization explains, "The first step toward changing this dire situation for the better is developing an understanding of the issue." This social experiment "provides an opportunity to experience one challenge of living in extreme poverty—the challenge of getting enough to eat."[4] It also empowers activists to take action for something worth believing in.

And this commitment is just for five days. It's a personal expression of solidarity with the rest of the world to better understand what it may feel like eating only rice, beans, and water for each meal. People living this way are short on caffeine and never completely full of food. Always wanting more. And our water is clean, which is an even better situation than most.

Much like this experiment, I broke down my math to compare my excess with the suffering. Let's assume for a moment that each meal that I eat costs only $1.25 per day. Let's also assume that one of my meals could feed a person caught in extreme poverty for one day. That means that the food I have in excess is 147 times that of some of the poorest people in the world. Once I began to quantify the excess of my kitchen pantry, it tweaked my desires. I found myself asking, "Why would I want more, when I already have much more than so many others in the world?"

STUCK IN THE MIDDLE

We've been overtaken by the push to acquire more than what is adequate. All the while, other people suffer. Global income inequality boggles the mind. Currently, the richest 1 percent of the world own as much collective wealth as the bottom 57 percent combined.

What do you think of this statistic?

I once stumbled upon an interactive website that quantifies your salary in contrast to the entire world. The quantitative tool was called "The Global Rich List," and I've summarized the results in a chart below (unfortunately, the site itself is no longer active). If you have never walked through this simple application of awareness before, take a look at the chart and consider how you stack up in comparison to the rest of the world. Are you surprised? Overwhelmed? Indifferent?

$2,500 annual income =
you are in the top **14.93** percent richest people in the world

$5,000 annual income =
you are in the top **14.39** percent richest people in the world

$10,000 annual income =
you are in the top **13.31** percent richest people in the world

$20,000 annual income =
you are in the top **11.16** percent richest people in the world

$30,000 annual income =
you are in the top **7.16** percent richest people in the world

$40,000 annual income =
you are in the top **3.17** percent richest people in the world

$50,000 annual income =
you are in the top **0.98** percent richest people in the world

$60,000 annual income =
you are in the top **0.91** percent richest people in the world

$80,000 annual income =
you are in the top **0.78** percent richest people in the world

$100,000 annual income =
you are in the top **0.66** percent richest people in the world[5]

Seeing this massive contrast between the rich and the poor can be disheartening. The greatest response to these statistics is to err toward the positive opportunity for generosity. Many people see these statistics as polarizing and impractical. Others think this information is just propaganda. My first response when I reviewed these statistics was simply to justify the percentages. For example, the cost of living is different across the globe. I work hard, and I deserve what I make.

Can I do something else with this information, other than moving on past the shock? Statistics are just numbers that are difficult to translate to our everyday lives. Part of the solution comes from meeting living, breathing examples of statistics that stick with us; we need a relatable person to make the numbers real. When we don't have a name and a face confronting us every day, when we don't have a Clarence looking into our eyes, we won't see things differently. It will not be as important to care for the needs of others. When we picture a person's face and say his or her name, we're connected to that person in a way that causes change. We will feel compelled to help, not out of guilt but out of relationship.

The contrast between the life I live and the life of my neighbor Clarence was just one example of this vast gulf that exists here in our own culture. Seeing the contrast between luxury and need in my life has been important as I consider the excess given to me. I have luxury. But how do I move from luxury to generosity? I must create new habits that challenge my view of enough by forcing me to look through the lens of the suffering and therefore cause me to reexamine my personal lifestyle of excess.

MONEY TALKS

A few years ago we had a frank conversation about money with a group of friends. We tackled what most of middle-class America considers a taboo subject, and because of the honesty in the room we faced some hard facts. We realized that our close-knit community's habits negatively influenced the financial situation of our dearest friends. Our personal habits affected the people we love.

Eating out had become the cultural gathering point for our community. We went to church on Sunday morning, and the natural follow-up was to get some lunch together. It became our Sunday ritual. Church. Lunch. We love to eat together. Unfortunately, this seemingly innocent ritual of eating out caused some friends to increase their personal indebtedness to the credit-card companies.

How did we get to this point?

Some may read this and put the blame on others. "They should have told you." But in their defense, that's a deeply embarrassing conversation, and we always used what we considered playful peer pressure to convince them to join us. The real issue is that we had taken two genuine needs (food and friendship) and chosen a luxury (going out to eat) as a way to fulfill those needs. As we walked through this conversation openly and honestly over time, all of our lifestyles changed. The truth was, none of us really cared about going out to eat; we all just wanted to be together for a meal. We all loved hanging out together. We all needed to eat. We did not, however, need to go out to an expensive restaurant in order to fill those needs.

So instead we put our heads together, set aside individual agendas, and got creative. Those of us who had extra income chose to see it from someone else's perspective, and all of us took the opportunity to forge a new way. We began having lunches together at one house, and everyone would bring a dish to pass around and share. Or sometimes, instead of hanging out over a lunch, we would gather for games and dessert later in the evening. Our friendships reached a new depth because we placed a higher value on community over convenience. Plus, we had a community that shared honestly about our needs.

Is this a conversation you have ever engaged with your closest friends? You may want to consider asking them what lifestyle choices you currently practice that influence their decision-making. The very thought of this conversation probably makes you twitch uncomfortably as you read, but it takes honest conversation for great friends to grow even closer.

INVITE A CONVERSATION

The community most difficult to relate to is the one furthest from your current financial situation. It's difficult to practically relate the reality of my food pantry to a boy starving in Somalia. It's hard to make sense of the contrast between the amount of meals that I can eat out of my freezer and the suffering of Mayan widows and their children in Guatemala. The conversation becomes much more approachable and personal when I relate it to my best friends who I have lunch with every Sunday. In order to challenge our perceptions of enough and to consider where to draw a line for our personal story, we need to look through the lens of those closest to us, as well as the lens of the broadest people groups possible.

Relationships similar and different can radically change our mind-set—can change you and me, can change our families, communities, and places of work. Changing our perspectives and opening up communication about our habits of eating out regularly is not something we can easily understand alone.

As you continue reading, I'd like to challenge you to consider whom you could invite to read this book *with* you. In order to change our current habits, we must become individuals and communities willing to rise up and question our current understanding of excess. It can be difficult to do this alone. Who do you trust to help you answer your question of "What is enough" for you? Whom do you know who can speak truth into your life but also try something new alongside you? With whom do you want to partner to dream up a new way of living and a new way of serving? Our communities can ask new questions and respond with creative solutions. We won't change without the help of others, and many conversations must occur before that change can become our ethos of living.

And yet, the change still begins with me. Take a risk. Ask someone to walk this journey with you.

But don't stop there.

Consider for a moment someone you know whose place on the scale of enough is much closer to the "needing more" end. Do you have any friends who challenge your way of life simply by their presence in your life? Or have societal walls sheltered you from knowing anyone significantly different from you?

Statistics are one thing, but friends are another. Numbers may challenge your mind, but faces will soften your heart. And names will stick with you over time. What are you willing to change in your everyday scenery to make a personal connection with someone who may be in need? This can be tricky. But the process may simply start with talking with someone who exhibits a generous spirit, with listening to his or her stories. Maybe you start to consistently read a blog by someone serving a specific people group in a third-world country or even the homeless in your community. Try walking next door and striking up a conversation with your neighbor. You know what will push your comfort zone just enough. And I trust that a still, small voice will guide you in this process. Our definitions of enough and our willingness to share are best served through relationships.

ENOUGH TALK

Everyone agrees that food is a basic and essential need for survival. One actionable thing that you can do today is to go into your kitchen pantry or cupboard and find five cans of food. Find the nearest food bank in your area. Deliver those five cans of food to the distribution location. Don't place the cans in a bin—deliver them to a person and have a conversation. Seek to see beyond the statistics and into the lives of those affected by hunger in your own community. Ask them about the food needs of your city. Find out how many children are hungry in your community. Learn everything you can about that food bank and how it addresses the needs of hunger in the place you live.

By doing this, you will learn something new, and it will make you think in a new way about your next meal. Lastly, talk about what you learned in this experience the next time you share a meal with a friend.

[4]

GOOD ENOUGH

The good you do today may be forgotten tomorrow.
Do good anyway. Give the world the best you have
and it may never be enough. Give your best anyway.
For you see, in the end, it is between you and God.
It was never between you and them anyway.

—*Mother Teresa*

There was once a stonecutter who was dissatisfied with himself and with his position in life.

One day he passed a wealthy merchant's house. Through the open gateway, he saw many fine possessions and important visitors.

How powerful that merchant must be! thought the stonecutter. He grew very envious and wished that he could be like the merchant.

To his great surprise, he suddenly became the merchant, enjoying more luxuries and power than he had ever imagined. Immediately, those less wealthy than him envied and detested him. Soon a high official passed by, carried in a sedan chair, accompanied by attendants and escorted by soldiers beating gongs. Everyone, no matter how wealthy, had to bow low before the procession.

How powerful that official is! he thought. *I wish that I could be a high official!*

Then he became the high official, carried everywhere in his embroidered sedan chair, feared and hated by people all around him. It was a hot summer day, so the official felt very uncomfortable in the sticky sedan chair. He looked up at the sun. It shone proudly in the sky, unaffected by his presence.

How powerful the sun is! he thought. *I wish that I could be the sun!*

Then he became the sun, shining fiercely down on everyone, scorching the fields, cursed by the farmers and laborers alike. But a huge black cloud moved between him and the earth, so that his light could no longer shine on everything below.

How powerful that storm cloud is! he thought. *I wish that I could be a cloud!*

Then he became the cloud, flooding the fields and villages, shouted at by everyone. But soon he found that he was being pushed away by some great force and realized that it was the wind.

How powerful it is! he thought. *I wish that I could be the wind!*

Then he became the wind, blowing tiles off the roofs of houses, uprooting trees, feared and hated by all below him. But after a while, he ran up against something that would not move, no matter how forcefully he blew against it—a huge, towering rock.

How powerful that rock is! he thought. *I wish that I could be a rock!*

Then he became the rock, more powerful than anything else on earth. But as he stood there, he heard the sound of a hammer pounding a chisel into the hard surface and felt himself being changed.

What could be more powerful than I, the rock? he thought. He looked down and saw far below him the figure of a stonecutter.

An unknown author wrote this story centuries ago, and its profound message rings true today. We all want to be something else—yet we truly can only be ourselves. The only thing I can ever be is me. I can't be you. I can't be Brad Pitt. I can't be any more charismatic or winsome. *I am me.* And because no other person can be me, I am good enough. You be you.[1] And because no other person can be you, you are good enough. We are better than enough.

People immediately form an opinion the first time they see a picture of themselves. Instantly upon looking at the image, they have summed up whether or not it is a good picture.

I've enjoyed several unique opportunities for creatively directing photo shoots. I had the privilege of leading a team of six photographers at a photojournalistic event, and I've also picked out and purchased clothes for a photo shoot with best-selling leadership guru John C. Maxwell. I've helped capture the streets of South Atlanta for a storybook project and led film shoots with the hope of changing childhood obesity.

Every photo-related project creates unforgettable stories. We used to joke that with an unlimited amount of money and unlimited amount of time, we can make anyone look like anything. Disney is very talented at creating such an experience. We can all visualize the radically edited photos on the covers of the magazines in the checkout lines. Changing reality to fit one vision or another has become the norm in our society, but changing the way we view our own image is never as easy as changing the filter on a camera.

Growing up, I felt great confidence when looking at pictures of myself. My parents encouraged me, and I never had self-esteem issues; on the contrary I had issues due to overconfidence. Growing up, I had an inflated view of myself, and people knew me as cocky and conceited at times. But something happened in my twenties. The way I viewed myself started shifting. I didn't notice it at first. I began playing a game in my head, comparing myself with those around me. I tried to quantify my self-worth. My self-worth became proportionate to how much stuff I had and how it adorned me. I didn't realize the problem for a long time. The problem became apparent to me through photographs, but by the time I recognized what had happened, I'd traveled a long way down the path of comparison, and this struggle carried along unintended consequences.

Jon Acuff said it so clearly: "Success will tell you that your enough is not enough, and it will keep you on a treadmill of your own design, but a treadmill nonetheless. Instead of chasing enough, you have to define it. If you chase it you'll never catch it. Enough is incredibly quick. Much like perfection, it seems to remain out of reach."[2]

I am an early adopter of most technological developments, especially if it has a creative or marketing bent. So I joined Facebook early on in its development.

There are many aspects of social media that I love, and it's become a great tool to connect with people and get feedback on new projects we've started. There are also some negative aspects to social networking. It's the first time in our society when we have been able to quantify our number of followers and, often, misrepresent that number as equaling influence. The thing that I dislike most about Facebook is photo tagging—the process of sharing photos. Someone can select you in a photo and attach your name to it for everyone to see. Tagging can be great fun, but it can also be a great problem.

Soon after joining Facebook, I got tagged, tagged, and tagged again. While every Facebook friendship requires approval, at the beginning there was no approval process for the posting of photos. So whether I liked it or not, I got tagged.

It was a joke at the start. Friends would post pictures and tag me, and I would untag myself. Tag. Untag. Tag. Untag. Close friends of mine all know that I get very frustrated by the photo tagging feature, so they would make sure that I was tagged in more than my share just to push my buttons.

As Facebook alerted me to these photos, I immediately checked them out. I told myself that each picture was a bad picture of me and would untag myself. Over and over again. Andre posted family pictures, and I explained what a bad picture I thought she shared. Two years went by in which I thought I looked horrible in every picture. I remember one of the last times this happened with Andre. She showed me her latest picture, and again, I responded that it was a bad picture. But she loved it. For some reason, emotion overwhelmed me, and it finally broke through. I broke down into tears of frustration and embarrassment.

It hit me. It wasn't the picture that was the problem; it was me. I didn't like *me*. I didn't like how I looked. I didn't look good enough. I didn't compare. I wanted to be something else or someone else.

My hair wasn't right. My smile wasn't that cool smirk that I desired. My teeth weren't white anymore, thanks to too much coffee drinking. My face was getting a little wider from not working out. My shirt wasn't right. I have a constant wrinkle between my eyes. I critiqued every element of myself. This was the image I saw of myself through my eyes—ultimately, I had a skewed self-image.

Since then I've embarked on a journey of rediscovering the uniqueness of who I am and becoming content with that person. This journey of believing my life matters and is important has revealed some valuable lessons.

IMAGE LESSONS

Personal Adequacy Is the Beginning
to Understanding Enough

I never saw myself as enough. I looked in the mirror and missed what was good. Instead of seeing what I contributed to the world, I only saw what I didn't have compared with others. I had a constant editorial eye on the real me. The truth is that my unique contribution to humanity is too important for me to see only my facade in a photo. I missed how unique I am. I wanted a faux me, which in the end offered a fictional contribution to a real world. I have a gift waiting to be presented and shared. I think a lot of us feel this way, but we are more than adequate; each of us is important.

Only You Living Your Designed Purpose Will Change the World

As I struggled with my personal adequacy, I began to neglect my important contribution to my closest friends. I saw what I didn't have that others had, while my friends saw the gifts I possessed that I wasn't using for their betterment. I wanted to be something different, and my friends just wanted me to be me. Other people need me; they don't need some persona that I want to be. Some of my friends explained to me that I shortchanged them of my role in their lives. I was not living the story that I needed to share with those around me. You see, if we never accept our true selves, we will always come up short on what we can become and how that could shape the lives of others.

Too often we quantify self-worth through possessions or image, but our worth should be found through living out our strengths in the most complete way. Nothing we have in the form of material value will ever be adequate to fulfill that need. No thing we gain will ever be good enough. Our presence lived fully is always of greater value than anything draped over it. Products always have short shelf lives; but our presence in our communities, blemishes and all, will last and has the opportunity to influence people we love every day. Your identity is not a trend; it is an essential element in all of our lives.

Dr. Martin Luther King Jr. explained this thought perfectly:

> All life is interrelated.... We are caught in an inescapable network of mutuality; tied in a single garment of destiny.... Strangely enough, I can never be what I ought to be until you are what you ought to be. You can never be what you ought to be until I am what I ought to be. This is the way the world is made. I didn't make it that way, but this is the interrelated structure of reality.[3]

By design, we must fully live the life that only we can live. Every person that lives less than his or her potential is limiting all human potential because that person is not offering the world the fullness of his or her true self.

Identity Is Incomparable

For the first time in history, we have the tools for anyone to see how they numerically measure up to others. We have analytics for the people who like and read each of our blog posts.[4] We can compare web traffic on our sites to every other site in the world. We can count the number of people who share our ideas with their communities.

There is even a way to quantify social-media influence.[5] Everything on the web now quantifies influence and popularity.

I recently talked to a popular blogger who felt frustrated about moving down on a list from #2 to #13. So, immediately I asked:

"Is that a list where you want to be number one?"

He responded quickly, "No, I don't care at all about that list."

Losing popularity on a list that he didn't even care about in the first place frustrated him. He felt his value diminish, without even stepping back to realize that that value was not of value to his values.

Understanding our value to the world can never be quantified through social attention in this way. Only you can contribute what only you can give to the world. Never let rankings or numbers of "likes" determine who you are and what you should do with your life. This false understanding of your identity does not define what you have to contribute to the world. You cannot be compared with others. There is only one of me. There is only one of you.

Tom Patterson said, "When you discover and use your gifts for the good of those you love and have chosen to serve, your life takes on beauty. It inspires others. It points toward the Creator."[6]

We Need More of You

If we do not fully value and live out who we were designed to be, we limit what we can contribute to society. Imagine our loss if Michelangelo never created his masterpieces, if Thomas Edison never shared the lightbulb, if Rosa Parks did not have the courage to sit in that seat on the bus, if Michael Jordan never displayed his running dunk from the free-throw line, if Anne Frank didn't write those pages of her journal, or if George Lucas never told the story of *Star Wars*. Our society would lack the incredible inspiration each of these people offered the world. If they never shared their gifts with us, we would not be the same.

Steven Pressfield makes a great point related to this important role and how it affects our understanding of ourselves in his masterful book *The War of Art*: "Creative work is not a selfish act or a bid for attention on the part of the actor. It's a gift to the world and every being in it. Don't cheat us of your contribution. Give us what you've got."[7]

When you freely give your art to the world, the world will respond with a standing ovation. Be you. As my friend Brian graffitis on huge brick walls and rooftops as a reminder to people that are struggling: "You are beautiful."

Believing You Matter Will Be a Lifelong Journey

Let me reassure you, it didn't change for me all in one day. I didn't suddenly become a self-confident person or view myself in a healthy way overnight. It took a lot of comparing to rob me of my confidence, and it took a lot of retraining to change my self-image. Mike Foster said, "The sooner we recognize human life is important—*period*—the sooner our lives start to feel more humane."[8] Every single day I struggle with the view through which I see others and myself. As I grow older, I see a few gray hairs, it's harder to stay in shape, and I am realizing that these wrinkles will forever be etched on my face. The things I see in the mirror will continue to change. The question I have to answer is, "How will I respond to what I see?"

Eryn Erickson is a singer and songwriter for a band called EDDY, and she's been on a similar journey. She wrote, "I was just a little girl in a small town where everyone had an opinion of who you should be. I saw the struggle to meet the impossible standards for success set by the media and reinforced by peer pressure; but I also saw the strength that can be drawn from the support of your family and people who love you. Struggling with the unfair expectations put on you is something you don't have to do alone."[9]

Eryn overcame her self-doubt and is going after her dream. Along the way, she started a community to help people overcome the pressure of society and to empower people to pursue their dreams. She named this community "So Worth Loving," a statement that embodies her comfort in her identity. She recently had the words tattooed on her forearm because she knows that whether the community exists forever or not, this will be a reminder of how to view herself. The doubts will always come back, but the statement gives her confidence.

You and I both need to believe that we have more to do and become, and in this process we will begin to find the truth: *we are good enough.*

Celebrating Others' Uniqueness Will
Encourage Your Personal Identity

Katie has no hair. At age two, she lost her hair and was diagnosed with alopecia totalis[10], an autoimmune disorder that causes total body hair loss. She has not had hair since. For about twenty-five years, she wore a wig to cover up her condition. Her mother encouraged her to wear a wig, fearing the cruel things other children might say to her. A very reasonable concern. One day we went to Six Flags with Katie and her husband, Josh. While we were in line awaiting the death-defying Superman ride, Katie was concerned that we would notice movement in her wig, so she decided to share her story with us to shield herself from any future embarrassment. Katie educated all of us that day, and this moment of vulnerability became the start to one of our best friendships in life.

Katie never had a problem explaining her story to others, but she always drew a line when openly revealing her true self. Every time she wore her wig, it acted as a shield from the public. Her wig was a safety net. In some ways it just removed the questions; in other ways it didn't let her fully live the life she was designed to live.

One day, Andre begged Katie not to wear her wig, and she was beautiful. Her head was perfect. Being bald is truly who she is, and there is no shame in sharing this story with others. She revealed her identity more and more over time, until one day she chose to get rid of her wig altogether. The problem wasn't the wig itself—the problem was that, like me, she didn't view her identity as adequate and important to her role in a greater story.

Over the course of two years, Katie started to see herself with new eyes. She believed she was good enough. She realized that her story is unique and important to share with others. She is perfect and beautiful. Her true self began to emerge, and a confidence revealed itself. Katie is a determined soul who cares for others and makes people feel great about themselves. Her personal journey of coming to a place of confidence made her the trusted confidante of many struggling with their own identities.

To say that understanding you are good enough is important would be an understatement. You are good enough. Let me repeat that statement: you *are* good enough. You don't need more stuff, you don't need a makeover, you don't need a wig— you just need to be everything you are designed to be. You are "so worth loving." Until you believe this important truth, you will never have the opportunity to contribute to the greater needs in our world.

To whom do you compare yourself? What story do you wish to live? Where do you imagine yourself in ten years? What are you doing to sell yourself short of that goal?

Your story will not be the same as that of anyone else on the planet. You are unique. That is the best part. To determine what is enough, we must become confident with our own answer to the question. If we do not believe we *are* good enough, we will never *have* enough.

● *Visual Moment*
Watch Katie's story: www.moreorlessbook.com/#videos

ENOUGH TALK

I remember a couple months after my photograph epiphany, my friend Mike Foster, a creative mind who founded People of the Second Chance[11], started a social experiment through his Facebook profile page. Mike posted a picture of himself that he took the moment he got out of bed. He wrote a note to go along with it, asking others to post the "real you." No touch-up on the photos, no makeup in the morning, no showers to look better, no gunk in your hair, and no brushing your teeth. Wake up and take a photo and post it online as a rare, honest statement of the real you. Be true to who you are.

This was the first social experiment that I chose not to participate in. It was too difficult. I hadn't overcome this phobia in my life quite yet. But as I watched it play out, I experienced freedom within my own life as others freely shared their photos. If you've never tried this for yourself, I would encourage you to do it. In an age of digital personas, we want both to hide ourselves and to be accepted for all that we are. This may be a simple start to pursuing an authentic you.

[5]

ENOUGH CLOTHING

> The people who make our clothes are poor. We are
> rich. It's natural to feel guilty, but guilt or apathy or
> rejection of the system does nothing to help.... This
> quest is about the way *we* live and the way *they* live;
> because when it comes to clothing, others make it,
> and we have it made. And there's a big, big difference.
>
> —*Kelsey Timmerman,* Where Am I Wearing?

It was a cold and dark night as the rain pelted our roof. Earlier that evening I had looked up at the overflowing gutter system on our house and thought that it was a really bad storm. The rain was not going to let up for a long time. My wife and I were inside our warm home with the lights dimmed as we drank coffee, ate dessert, and played an intense game of Settlers of Catan. When you play a game like this, everything else happening in the world seems to stop.

The doorbell rang. It was Clarence.

Andre opened the door to find him wearing a simple black rain jacket with the hood over his head. Rain completely soaked his body from head to toe. You know the feeling, when every single piece of clothing on your body suction-cups to your skin? It's like walking around engulfed in a wet mop. Sometimes when it rained, Clarence's relatives in the area would let him hang out at their house until the storm passed. The park has a picnic area that some people without a home slept under, but that dry space has strong territorial boundaries in the neighborhood, and Clarence wasn't known for the way he made friends with others on the streets. That night he had no place to go. Before he rang my doorbell, I hadn't given a second thought to how he might spend this night. He had no food, no dry clothes, and no place to call home. On nights like this, he would just keep walking to try and stay warm. To this day, during a big storm Andre and I remember the downtrodden look on Clarence's face. He was heartbroken and exhausted.

We instantly took off his jacket, and he started wringing out his shirt. We asked him what he wanted. He didn't want to come in the house. He never did. He always had a dignified air about him, and we never pushed him or told him what he needed; rather, we let him drive the conversation and tried to be compassionate friends who upheld that dignity. Standing in our doorway, he asked us for three things. First, some dry clothes. Second, one of those McDonald's gift cards we had given him in the past. Third, if it got bad again, could he stay on our porch? How could we possibly say no to any of these basic needs of clothing, food, and shelter?

I stepped away from the door and walked to my closet. My closet is a square room about five feet by five feet in size with its own door. Suddenly, that closet seemed a bit ridiculous. It would have been much more than imaginable to Clarence. I opened my drawer and pulled out a pair of socks (I owned more than twenty), grabbed some underwear (maybe fifteen in the drawer), pulled out a T-shirt (I probably get twenty-five annually from events I help organize), a rain jacket, and a pair of jeans. Then I looked down at my shoes. I owned thirteen pairs, and five were different styles of athletic shoes. I grabbed a pair of Nikes and ran back to the front door. To me, this was a quick, painless cleaning out of my closet. By the look on Clarence's face, I handed him diamonds on a night when everything around him had turned to coal.

Next was the gift card. A ten-dollar McDonald's gift card meant a ton of money to my friend and meant nothing to me. Tara Struyk stated the situation perfectly: "When it comes to the way we think about money, I've noticed there are two kinds of people: those who think $1,000 is a lot of money, and those who think $10 is a lot of money."[1] To my friend, that gift card meant more than simply food and drink. Clarence had educated me during a different conversation; any fast-food chain on a stormy night represented a warm place to sit down for a few hours, get cleaned up, and use the restroom. Walking up to the counter with money in his hand gave Clarence leverage to get what he needed, and they wouldn't ask him to leave for a few hours.

Self-reflection was both natural and essential that night. I had no idea how many pieces of clothing I owned. I quickly realized, though, that if at any time anyone asked me for the shirt off my back, I had another one to replace it. And if I didn't, I could get another one at the store without thinking twice. I decided at that moment that if Clarence ever needed clothes, I would give to him freely. He asked for socks consistently because his socks quickly became wet from sweat and rain. He often received new T-shirts from me. Over time, he became like a walking neighborhood billboard for any project or event I'd helped organize the previous year. He had one bright orange shirt that a friend recognized a mile away. He wore that orange crush color with pride, and I could never pull off that color the way he did. Some people may read this and not agree with giving handouts to Clarence, but I never thought of it as a handout. It was more like giving to a friend. This situation, in my mind, was similar to a neighbor who needs a little bit of sugar to finish off a cookie recipe. Over time, we gained a mutual respect for each other, so my gifts to him were not out of pity; they were an outflow of our relationship.[2]

Standing in my closet that evening, it was obvious: I have more than enough clothes. Clothes are a basic necessity, so it's easy for us to justify having a lot of them. But how did I get so many? As I analyzed my more-than-full collection, I found that many of my clothes fit into one of the following categories.

CATEGORIES OF EXCESS

"Just in Case" Jackets

This question always comes up when I pack for a trip: *what should I bring?* I ponder what the weather will be, or if there will be any dress-up dinners. I always err on the safe side, just in case. Then I get home from the adventure and realize I could have taken out half the clothes that I originally packed.

Isn't that just a microstory of our entire wardrobe?

Before we realize it, we end up with a closet full of "just in case" clothes. Just in case your work holds that '80s party again this year. Just in case you take a trip to Alaska this year and need that pair of long underwear. Just in case someone passes away and you need to wear a suit and tie. Just in case sweater vests come back into style and you can wear them again. Just in case you decide to go on a cruise sometime in the next three years and could wear that formal pink dress that your sister made all the bridesmaids buy for her wedding. Just in case high heels become the standard at work. Just in case you decide to go on a service trip and they tell everyone to wear scrubs. Just in case you lose or gain ten pounds.

"Just in case" clothes can take up a lot of extra space. *We could probably do with less.*

"Free" T-shirts

Growing up in Michigan, my friend Jeff and I attended countless sporting events. We're both big Michigan State Spartan fans and went to many hockey, basketball, and football games. Sometimes we took a road trip to Detroit for a Red Wings, Lions, or Tigers game.

One thing was certain: we always came home with a free T-shirt—it was our trophy at the end of the day. Marketers must love kids like us. At most games your options are either to catch a T-shirt from a rally team entertaining the crowd during breaks in gameplay, or to sign up for a free T-shirt and register for a credit card at the same time. I didn't think much of it as a clueless sixteen-year-old as I registered over and over again. The credit-card companies know that the earlier they get a person using their brand, the greater likelihood of that person using that same credit card for the rest of their life.[3]

Fast-forward ten years. We got a credit check for our first home mortgage, and I had twenty-one open credit cards. Huh? I only use one credit card. I didn't remember signing up for those. I don't have a wallet big enough to hold twenty-one credit cards. I guess those free T-shirts weren't free after all, and apparently I wasn't the only one who got sucked into those credit card schemes. In 2009 a law went into effect to curb these free T-shirt fiascos.[4]

I met a guy in Charlotte who was engaged, and his soon-to-be wife had declared that he had to get rid of his T-shirt collection. He staged a countdown to the wedding by wearing every T-shirt in his closet one time, and then he gave them all away to a local thrift store. When he tallied up all of his T-shirts, he had over 150. He got most of them for free as prizes, from sports teams, or from his local church to promote the latest sermon series. Why is it that we're all suckers for a free T-shirt?

There's a new social media strategy called IWearYourShirt.com[5] created by Jason Sadler, who understands that T-shirts are a market-ing strategy in today's society. The concept is simple. You pay him money, and he wears your shirt. He has recruited a team of people to enhance his reach across the nation. They wear the T-shirt. They will create a video for online promotion, post photos of themselves wearing the shirt online to social media sites, and live stream it all. It just goes to show that T-shirts have become a marketing engine in our culture, and we are consumed by it. Does a shirt have anything to do with purchasing power? Jason's perspective is enlightening: "You don't buy something because you saw it on a billboard. You buy things because your friends tell you to."[6] When we wear something, we physically give our personal endorsement to the story that we're wearing and broadcasting. We *become* a promotion. Do you fully approve of the messages you communicate through your clothes?

"Spring Green" Sweaters

Most of us have clothes for certain weather, which is both understandable and essential. But are your seasonal clothes determined by color? In the 1950s someone developed a color chart that trained consumers to determine what colors are acceptable to wear in what seasons. As the seasons change the colors in nature change, but I'm not sure it's necessary for us to change our clothing as well. It amazes me how strongly "Never wear white past Labor Day" is ingrained in our minds. Of course, fashion designers and retailers love to encourage us in this mental exercise by constantly changing the "in" color for each season and each year. No one wants to get caught wearing last year's mint green during this year's spring green season.

There is a store in the Nashville area called Billy Reid, which is one of many clothing stores that plays up this concern with buyers. Stores like these often invite their best customers to come for the launch of new seasonal clothing lines before the general public can buy them.[7] Billy Reid makes very quality clothing with a unique style that is capturing the attention of fashion experts globally.

Bill Hampton is a successful executive in the area who always dresses with great precision and style, and he always gets invited to attend this exclusive gathering at Billy Reid. For over a year now, Bill has been practicing forty-day challenges to change his worldview and shift his perspective on many aspects of life. One particular month, he chose not to buy any clothes. Of course, one week into his break from purchasing clothing he received the exclusive invitation to attend the fall clothing release party at Billy Reid. On one hand, he naturally wanted to go to the event. On the other he had committed to this lifestyle for one month. The fortuitous timing of these two events helped him to realize how the draw of fashion consumed his actions. He chose that year not to attend and felt for the first time that the marketing draw of the industry wasn't driving his decision-making. Just to be clear, Billy Reid is not doing things wrong. They have a strong marketing strategy, but if we as consumers do not understand what marketing does to us, we are not defining what is enough; we are letting others determine the definition for us. Does the pull of new clothes for a new season influence your decision-making and purchasing power?

"Dress to Impress" Suits or Dresses

Special occasions often cause us to buy new clothing. An office Christmas party. A wedding. A hot date. If something out of the ordinary or exciting is going on, we create an excuse to get a new outfit. Growing up as the pastor's kids, my siblings and I always got new clothes for Easter Sunday morning, and we dressed up every Sunday.

My sister Joanna once tested this rule in a sociology class experiment. The challenge was to think of a situation and/or setting and determine an action that would be considered deviant in that setting. Then she had to act it out. In her words, "Having grown up as a pastor's kid, most of my life I lived with the awareness that I was living in a bubble. It felt like whatever I did, said, or even wore would be quickly analyzed and often judged as evidence of how poorly or well my parents were raising me." Having been off at college and enjoying freedom, she chose our home church as the setting for her deviant experiment.

"I showed up one Sunday morning in my oldest sweatpants and sweatshirt," my sister wrote. "No notice to my parents. And I was not allowed to give an explanation of my behavior during the experiment. Now I had always thought my church was quite accepting of those from varying socioeconomic backgrounds. It was quite normal to have a homeless person wander in and out, and we had many poor and working class families who regularly attended. However, the standard for the pastor's family was obviously high. I got all kinds of comments and funny looks."

Some of the responses that day were imaginative. "What? Have you been camping this weekend?" "Left all your clothes on campus?" "Nice to see you dressed up today." Her favorite, honestly, was from a family member who simply came up and said, "I'm sure you have a good explanation for this and that it will not happen again, right?"

Part of the experiment required her to debrief about how she felt throughout the experiment. "I felt varying levels of embarrassment, anger, shame, and righteous indignation. Not being able to explain myself, to give a reason for my appearance made me feel powerless. I stuck out like a sore thumb and had no defense mechanism. Though I expected to make some waves, the emotional responses both externally and internally surprised me."

Our clothes can be used to impress others and instill confidence fueled by how good we think we look, and our clothes can very well do the opposite. A question to consider: how often have I bought an outfit to impress for an occasion and never worn it again?

Look At My Unique/Cool/Cute Shoes

The biggest reason we want to buy new clothes is because we want to look good. And we want people to notice that we look good. In short, we want attention. We see unique/cool/cute shoes, and we want to wear them because someone, somewhere will tell us we have unique/cool/cute shoes on and make us feel good about ourselves. When we have new clothes on, we feel better about ourselves.

"Do Good" Necklaces

"It's for a good cause." *Right?* How many times have we used this expression when purchasing a T-shirt, beaded necklace, handmade bracelet, shoes, or specialty bag? Purchasing a product that supports a charity does not ease an addiction to clothing; rather it extends the addiction and tries to make us feel good about spending more money. Our organization, Plywood People, sells products that create jobs for refugees, and I believe these products are a better purchasing option than other consumer products. Why? We use upcycled materials, pay fair wages to the artisans, and help lift people out of poverty. However, just because a product helps a charity does not mean that you need to overspend in order to buy it.

Conscious consumerism is good—and it is bad. It is good because in a small way it makes the world a better place and improves lives. It is bad because it's become the latest marketing angle, causing us to buy more than we need. As it relates to clothing, we need to keep our guard up and determine whether we need the product, want the product, or simply want to support the charity and have no need for the product at all.

My closet was filled with all those clothes and more. Once again, coming to terms with the truth made me uncomfortable because

I like clothes. They make me feel good about myself. They offer security for all the possible scenarios I may encounter. They draw attention. However, they can also go beyond necessity and begin to define who I am and how I feel.

WE ARE NOT OUR CLOTHES

While I was processing all of this, I met Ashley Nienaber on a spring break service trip called The Original Event in Galveston, Texas. At the event we gathered about 250 college students to help rebuild homes destroyed along the coast from Hurricane Ike (and yes, I did receive a free T-shirt for being there). Ashley and I led the event along with the host organization, Mission Year.[8] Mission Year team members choose to give a year of their life to serve in an urban context. I told her about the experience we had with our kitchen pantry, which encouraged her to tell me about a project she'd been dreaming about.

The idea came to her while riding a bus through the inner city of Chicago. She had been in the area for only a few months and traveled this route many times, but this trip she noticed something different.

As she looked out the bus window she suddenly became aware of how some of the people in the neighborhood were dressed. Some wore clothes that didn't fit right. Others' clothing appeared in need of a good wash. Some may have, out of necessity, had to wear the same shirt and pants for a few days or even to bed at night. She knew her neighbors and had seen them in these same outfits day after day, but for the first time it became clear to her what little choice they had regarding their clothing.

Her story was different. She could choose what outfits she wanted to wear and buy. Ashley realized that in her neighborhood, her freedom to choose her wardrobe put her in the minority among many of her neighbors.

Clothing had always played a significant role in Ashley's life. From shopping with friends to the excitement of wearing new outfits to sorority events, clothing had greatly determined her social and personal life. When she took the time to think about her relationship with clothing, it became obvious that her choice of jeans, T-shirts, or shoes each day typically conveyed an idea or status symbol. Like you and me, she owns professional outfits, workout clothes, clothing for spending time with friends, clothing for going out on dates, seasonal clothes, clothes for lounging around the house, and clothing for special occasions, such as weddings or funerals. Her clothes weren't just necessity anymore; they defined her.

Following that bus ride through Chicago, Ashley wanted to change her perspective toward clothes. Instead of continuing the lifestyle she had always lived and wearing the clothes she had always worn, she decided to challenge both herself and the powerful culture of clothing that had unknowingly overtaken her.

She conducted a social experiment focused on clothing and the role it played in her day-to-day life. For the duration of the experiment, she wore every article of clothing in her closet one time. The goal was to see how many days she could last without wearing one article of clothing a second time. She wanted to make herself question the reason behind what she wore every day and acknowledge the role clothing played in her life. Why is this pair of jeans her favorite? Why does she hate this pair of shoes? And why are they still in her closet?

She also wanted to challenge the freedom she experienced each day. So she decided that she would not be allowed to change clothes at all during the day, such as wearing one outfit for work and a different one for an evening out with friends. This forced her to plan ahead and dress accordingly for all the activities of the day. By limiting her freedom of clothing choice, she hoped to challenge her identity and learn how to function in society without the status symbols she had relied so heavily on before. She named her experiment as an anthem for her to never forget: "I am not my clothes."

Before the experiment began, she set a few other guidelines. For starters, she refrained from purchasing any new articles of clothing during the experiment. Also, she could not get rid of or donate any clothes before the experiment started. She was tempted to toss out all the items of clothing that were out of date, odd fitting, or just uncomfortable. But since others didn't have the choice, why should she? She would wear every item of clothing she owned, liked or not, and hopefully this social experiment would teach her how clothing influenced her daily life, both personally and socially.

By the time we met in Texas, Ashley was committed to conducting the social experiment. The only problem was that she hadn't started yet. How often is this the case for our own personal aspirations of change? *Too often.* As the famous Thomas Edison statement clearly communicates, "Genius is 1 percent inspiration, 99 percent perspiration." It takes courage to pursue an experiment like this, and we have to make the active choice to follow through.

I asked her how long she thought she could go without wearing the same thing twice. Her theory? She knew that she had many tops, so she thought she could last maybe seventy days in total. Which, at the time seemed like infinity. Imagine being able to go more than two months without wearing the same article of clothing twice. It seemed ridiculous until she embarked on her journey.

The "I Am Not My Clothes" experiment began. It started off pretty easy. Her first sets of clothes were her favorites. It got harder when she had to wear a wool sweater in the summer or sweatpants to work.

One hundred and fifty-six days later she was done. *ONE HUNDRED AND FIFTY-SIX.* That is more than twice the length she thought it would be and was the number of tops she wore during the experiment. Tops included shirts, dresses, sweaters, etc. (as you might imagine, bottoms and shoes did not last this long).

On the last day, she wore the final piece of clothing in her closet, the one she was dreading the most to wear: a full-length maroon bridesmaid dress. She handled it with grace as she arrived at her workplace that morning and finished that evening with fun by throwing a big celebration with her friends at a local bowling alley to celebrate her experience.

After the experiment I asked Ashley what would stick with her forever about her Enough Experiment.

She told me, "I had a hundred and ninety articles of clothing. The crazy thing is, I am someone who goes through my closet once or twice a year to donate stuff I don't wear anymore. I was shocked at how much I had. This project helped me realize how many pieces of clothing I own that I don't even like but I keep it 'as an option' or 'just in case.' When I was forced to wear my clothes, I realized that half of the time I actually felt uncomfortable in what I was wearing, either because it didn't really fit or I didn't really like it. So looking at this, I really only wear half of my clothes on a regular basis."

She went on to say that since her experiment, she buys clothes probably 70 percent less than she would have before, and out of the clothes that she's purchased, only 25 percent were new, while the rest were purchased from Goodwill, garage sales, and other secondhand options. It was an experience that changed Ashley and challenged everyone around her to think about what they wore and why.

Clarence changed the way I looked at my clothes. Ashley, Bill, and others gave me further reason to critically evaluate what I wear. While I haven't given up buying new clothes entirely, nor have I given up every extra pair of shoes, I have started to think before I buy. I have become more eager to give. I am aware of the ridiculous amount of stock I put into how my clothes make me feel and the attention I am hoping to receive from others. And I'm looking for more ways to use my excess to make a difference.

● *Visual Moment*
Watch Ashley's story: www.moreorlessbook.com/#videos

ENOUGH TALK

There is a good chance you will never go through the specific
Enough Experiment that Ashley developed, but there's an easy
way to replicate it. Go to your closet and drawers and pull out
every piece of clothing that you own. Count them. Sort them. We
created a worksheet that you can find in the back of the book or
download for free online to see "what is enough" for you and your
personal closet. Count every piece of clothing in your closet. How
many pairs of socks? How many undergarments? Shirts? Shoes?
Pants? Skirts? Dresses? How many days could you go without
wearing the same thing twice? Are you satisfied with your number,
or do you have an excess of clothing?

If you feel you have too much, then decide what is enough
for each category of clothing. Choose the ugliest piece of clothing
from your closet and cut a four-by-six-inch square out of it. Write
your personal "enough number" on that piece of clothing in a
black permanent marker. Frame it. Turn it into art. Hang it in your
bedroom. Make it a special number. *An unforgettable number.* This
keepsake will keep it *in* sight and *in* mind. Finally, sort through all
your clothing and pare down your clothes to meet your reasonable
number. Anything more than that number is excess. Call it what

it is, and change your equation. What follows are a few tips for choosing which clothes to release. Let it go:

- If you haven't worn the article of clothing in the past year.
- If you forgot you owned the item and just remembered again.
- If you have only worn the item once since it's been buried in your drawer or hanging in your closet.
- If you have to dream up a themed event that would be the perfect occasion to wear it.
- If you only kept the garment to please the person who gave it to you.

If you are like me, you probably have a bag full of clothes that you are unsure what to do with. I promise you will feel good about yourself when you look into a closet rid of excess. Remember, out of our excess we can address issues of need and suffering, so find a local shelter or clothing center and donate your excess. Live with less. Before you go to the clothing center, look in your closet and choose one piece of clothing that you truly love—and give that also. Don't only give your old but give your favorite, and you will begin to change your perspective toward clothing and live with a renewed hope through generosity.

[6]

ENOUGH PRESENTS

There are two ways to get enough: one
is to continue to accumulate more and
more. The other is to desire less.

—*G. K. Chesterton*

We readied ourselves to embark on the most gloriously selfish few hours of our lives, and we felt ecstatic. We held our guns in hand. The manager gave us the essential training, we filled out the form, and we gladly received our welcome packet. Everything was set for the big showdown, and it was just the two of us. The entire place stood before us, ours for the taking. This was our chance to add every single want and desire to the list.

That was the day we made our wedding registry at Target.

We started off slowly and selected towels. I really didn't have an opinion, but Andre had already chosen the colors and textures she desired in her head. My sisters gave us specific advice about towels: they told us to register for more than we thought we needed because they expected our home would often have visitors (they were right).

Next up, we moved toward the kitchen appliances. We selected a toaster. I already owned a toaster that I'd used all through college. Andre reminded me of this clearly, but I knew that toaster wasn't nice. I suggested we register for a new one, and she agreed.

My family had always used a large mixer to create the infamous Shinabarger Chocolate Chip Cookies. The mixer options were a two hundred and fifty dollar version that stood by itself with multiple mixing settings, a rotating bowl (with varying bowl sizes), and multiple mixing arm sizes depending on what you're making—or a hand mixer for twenty-five dollars. The choice was clear to me. The choice was clear to her. *We need the stand-up mixer*, I thought. But I was wrong. "Why would we ask someone to buy a two hundred and fifty dollar mixer for our wedding?" Andre asked rhetorically. She shot the tag of the simple hand mixer with her gun and continued walking. Moving on.

She wanted to register for a simple and cheap vacuum. I wanted the vacuum that would clean our home the best. We decided to ask some advice from friends and get back to this one. Then we took a break and registered for some DVDs. We both knew that my buddies would most likely want to buy these for us, so we each picked out five movies for our future collection. Then I moved over to the DVD player. I wanted the best one, while Andre wanted the cheapest. I wouldn't budge. She wouldn't budge. I said some hurtful things. She got mad. We stood in the middle of Target red-faced, bickering back and forth, registry guns in our hands, pointing back and forth at each other, neither of us listening to what the other wanted.

It was a stupid argument, but it became important. We did not see the world the same way, even though we had chosen to marry and see the world together for the rest of our lives. On this day, we looked at things very differently.

We quit the registry for that day and turned our guns back into the front desk.

We didn't get very far, but with this little exercise we entered into something far more important than any vacuum or toaster. As we walked through the parking lot that afternoon I remember some light flakes of snow falling, giving us a needed breather from the intensity of our conversation in the store. We were both very quiet.

We sat down in the front seats of the car, and I turned to Andre. What happened? Neither of us understood what had just transpired. So we began to share our stories. She started.

Her parents were missionaries. She was born in Bolivia and lived there until she was ten years old. They raised support to pay for everything in their lives during those years. They never knew what money would come in every month, which made every purchase important. This financial pressure was not Andre's responsibility to carry, but she assumed it by fully participating in purchasing decisions. They always purchased the least expensive option to make it to another month successfully. They focused on what was needed, not always what was wanted. Plus, Andre's dad is a handyman, and he often just fixed whatever wasn't working from the inside out. Therefore, the cheapest option was the wisest decision given their cash flow or lack thereof depending on the month.

My dad pastored a church, and my mom was an active leader in the church as well. I grew up in Lansing, Michigan, where my father worked at Central Free Methodist Church for seventeen years. Life was stable. The church steadily grew throughout that tenure. We bought things that would last. We usually purchased the most expensive option, counting on the item to last a very long time. My dad doesn't have a handy bone in his body. If something broke, it was always a major hassle to our family. When we made a purchase we usually bought the warranty, too, a guarantee that our purchase would last for the long haul.

WANTS VERSUS NEEDS

Andre and I see the world from two very different perspectives. Choosing gifts for our new life together introduced an issue far more complicated than we realized, forcing us to work through our pasts to engage a future of purchasing together. Honestly, we both had to make compromises moving forward. As the conversation progressed we began to ask some consistent questions that defined what we shot with our little Target gun: "What do we want, and what do we need? And to what level of desire are we comfortable with purchasing and sharing with our community to purchase for us?" Some things we registered for were purely *wants*. The DVD player we registered for was the best, and I clearly wanted it. We didn't need it, but it was pretty awesome when a family gifted that to us at our wedding. I didn't really *need* a fancy mixer, so we registered for the handheld mixer (and it still works well today, ten years later).

A need is something you must have, something you can't do without, such as water, food, shelter, and essential clothing. Needs will never go away, and they are essential to life day after day. When we think of others first, we most often seek to care for the basic needs of those *in need*. When I think back to our wedding registry, we didn't register for anything that was an essential need. The items on our list were accessories and tools to make living easier, but none were essential to our survival. A want is something you would like to have, but is not necessary for living. Wants are best related to desires. Wants are luxuries that adorn those things that we need.

The truth is that most of us living in American society in the twenty-first century have most of our needs met, and most of our wants as well. Sure, we all dream about some big desires that we'll never get like that awesome boat, the trip to Fiji, or the infinity pool in the backyard. But these are luxuries, and we should call them by name. I'm not saying that enjoying a luxury is wrong; I am simply naming it for what it is. Luxuries are gifts that we do not need or deserve. Luxuries are a treat for the owners and should be shared accordingly for others to enjoy freely. Even the idea of a wedding registry is clearly a luxury given only to a portion of us in the Western world.

It's common to use words like *need* and *want* interchangeably without thinking about it. We tend to use the word *need* more often than it is actually required. This is why having a healthy definition of these words can change how we live. When our wants start to dictate decisions, we should enact a reality check. We are rich. We have been given great opportunity in contrast to the broader world. Let me give you perspective. If you own a house, you are rich. If you own a car, you are rich. If you have ever been on a vacation, ever in your life, you are rich. If you own a computer, you are rich. If you own multiple outfits of clothing, you are rich. Chances are, if you are reading this book, you are rich.

We are rich.

We don't normally think of ourselves as rich, because we too often create a game of comparison. Someone who is rich is usually a person who is better off than me. We create a circle that is exclusive and usually not including ourselves.

When you're rich, you ask rich-people questions. Let me share an example. In the United States, when you meet a new person, generally the first thing you ask is: "What is your name?" The second question you ask is: "What do you do?"

The assumption is that you work.

Andre and I took extended time away from the US to write this book and dream about what our family ought to be for years to come. We chose to rent a house in Granada, Nicaragua. Nicaragua is unfortunately one of the poorest countries in Central America.[1] Granada is like a beautiful light in the midst of the country, very safe with generous and friendly people.

A woman cared for the rental house and offered to cook for us periodically (which was a great luxury). We enjoyed a great relationship with her over time, largely due to the fact that Andre speaks Spanish fluently. One night, she invited us to her home for dinner. Her home was small, but she cared for it perfectly, and she surprised us by introducing us to her fiancé. Andre translated for me when I asked him, "What do you do for work?"

Andre asked the question but later felt ashamed that we did.

He struggled to find work at the time. He was a driver for tourists, but times were tough. We made a rich-person assumption that he worked. Not all people have the opportunity of having a job, and this became very apparent to us in that moment.

We realized that evening as we talked about the situation that we had asked a rich-people question: a question that only rich people ask each other. These questions are not for all people, and this conversation was not inclusive of others. When we learn that our conversations are only geared toward the rich (or those similar to us), it's a chance to regain our perspective of needs, wants, and luxuries.

Andy Stanley talked about this in his sermon series entitled "How To Be Rich" at North Point Community Church. He made the entire audience repeat after him three times, "I have more than I need; I am rich." Then he coined a phrase, "Rich People Problems," that I am learning to integrate into my daily thinking.[2] Rich-people problems include:

- Running out of wrapping paper to wrap gifts.
- Figuring out where to put the money you're saving to pay for college after the kids leave home.

- Doing financial or estate planning because you're going to run out of time before you run out of money.
- Throwing away food because it spoiled before you could eat it.
- Using the downstairs kitchen for an extra week because the new counters, which are replacing perfectly usable but dated counters, did not come in on time.
- Replacing the electric door opener for your garage.
- Fighting with your family about how to use the weeks that you will get paid for not showing up for work.
- Feeling the need to write an entire chapter centered on clothes in a book about what is enough.

Yes, I am rich. And so are a good number of the people I interact with on a daily basis. This phrase is starting to catch on in our community. This language helps give perspective to our problems. And if you're still unsure about whether or not you are rich, let me help you. With all due respect to Jeff Foxworthy, here is my list. You might be rich if:

- You replace version 4 of your phone with version 5 of the same phone.

- You regularly change the color of the walls of your home.
- You have to decide which pair of shoes to wear today.
- You have a spare bedroom for guests to sleep in.
- Your pet is wearing the same outfit that you are wearing.
- You know what Wi-Fi means.
- Your therapist says, "Apple," and you say, "Computer."
- You push a button to dry clothes instead of waiting for the sun to appear.

I had a conversation one day with an executive from Kraft Foods. We talked about his division, which was the famous macaroni-and-cheese division. This man has a compassionate heart toward people in difficult economic situations. In his position, he learned so much about purchasing options. For example, he launched some new product lines of macaroni and cheese, including experimenting with flavor changes and noodle changes, which received an incredible response from middle- to upper-class markets but fell flat with the lower-income communities.

Why is that? Options are a rich person's problem. If I try out a new version of macaroni and cheese for the first time, it costs me one dollar. But if I don't like it, the worst-case scenario is that I just get something else from the refrigerator or run through a drive-thru. People who are purchasing out of an essential need or out of survival often can't afford the option of trying something new. If they don't like it, they don't eat. Or they have to grit their teeth and eat something they don't enjoy. The ability to choose is a great opportunity that many in the world have never experienced.

I believe that it's an extremely healthy practice to name rich-people problems in our community. When we start to define our problems in the context of the world around us, looking at needs, desires, and luxuries, our stress level falls exponentially, and we gain perspective. Rich-people problems don't cause us to suffer; rather they simply cause a setback in our modern, progress-filled life. These setbacks are often the biggest difference between the rich and the poor. We have a unique opportunity in those moments. When we identify rich-people problems, this gives us an opportunity to step back from our desires and luxuries and step foot into the shoes of those in need.

WHEN A GIFT IS NOT A GIFT

Have you ever given a present to a person because they gave you a present? I have many times. My dad calls this a "gift-for-a-gift gift." Someone was generous to us, so out of obligation we feel compelled to give a gift back. Our gift is a thank-you that we feel we ought to do as a response to another friend's generosity. When we receive the first gift, we get nervous because we didn't get them a gift. We go home and think about how we can make up for the gift that we received. What usually ends up happening is that we spend more than we normally would due to the guilt factor.

A gift-for-a-gift gift is not giving at all; rather, it is a response to the generosity of others. Generosity has a crazy way of *guilting* us into giving. Our act of giving turns into a requirement and doesn't signify any generosity at all. Generosity, on the other hand, is "the habit of giving freely without expecting anything in return."[3]

THE CHRISTMAS GIFT DILEMMA

You can't talk about presents without talking about Christmas, right? So how much is enough to spend on Christmas presents? There is no right answer. Hopefully, you're not reading this in December, because you're already in the thick of the purchasing dilemma.

Some friends started a great initiative a few years back called The Advent Conspiracy.[4] Several pastors realized that presents and gift giving had overtaken the true reason for Christmas. It was true in their families, in their churches, and across our nation. What if our families, churches, and country celebrated the reason for Christmas: the birth of Jesus? These pastors wanted to fully celebrate the reason for the season and worship the little child whose birth changed everything. What would happen to the gift scenario? How could these leaders challenge their congregations to choose to live a different story in the coming Christmas season? As a result, they challenged their communities to spend half of what they spent on Christmas in the previous year. So, if someone had spent a thousand dollars on gifts last year, they would choose to spend only five hundred dollars. Then they could give the difference to address issues of need and suffering. As a church community they would give that other half to clean-water initiatives around the world. The response was tremendous. They were able to give more.

It's not realistic to think that any of us are going to stop giving presents at Christmas. The truth is that we enjoy giving and receiving gifts. But has the gift-giving requirement overtaken true generosity? Are we giving out of love or giving out of demand? Do we need to give more to our own family, or could we look externally and give to needs in our communities? Has gift giving overtaken the greatest gift of the season? You might take the time to process these questions as a family in the next Christmas season.

THE FAMILY GIFT SOLUTION

I love to give presents. I also love to receive presents. As *The 5 Love Languages*[5] explained to me, I show love and experience love through gift giving. So I think a ton about gifts.

One of the gift-giving experiences that I've experienced as my family gets larger is the act of the family Christmas gift exchange. I don't know if your family has done this, but some people try to get many families to participate. Here is a truth: families grow, and as the family tree expands, it's harder to keep everyone connected.

In this exchange, everyone draws a name out of a hat and buys a present for someone else in the family at Christmas time. I buy a present for my cousin in Kansas. My cousin in Kansas buys a present for my uncle in Ohio. My uncle in Ohio buys a present for my sister in Michigan. My sister in Michigan buys a present for my aunt in Pennsylvania. My aunt in Pennsylvania sends a present to me in Georgia.

The idea is good, the intention is even better, but the results are a very small sense of connectivity and more stuff in our lives. What happens is we realize that we really don't know each other very well, so it's difficult to buy a present that our family member needs or even wants. Perhaps, we call a closer family member to determine something to buy that is close to the spending cap amount (usually around twenty-five dollars in our family).

As a family we try to stay connected through the act of purchasing something, but purchasing things doesn't unite anyone. Instead, what if your family united together to make a difference in the life of someone that needs help? Play this out with me. Let's say that your family gift exchange involves twenty-five people and the average gift costs twenty-five dollars, plus shipping. The total amount is thirty dollars per person. What if you collectively put that money together? And further, what if as a family you shared ideas for what you might do with that seven hundred and fifty dollars through email? What if each person shared a cause they were passionate about?

How awesome would it be to receive those emails, to learn about each family member's greatest passions? Then you set up a way for everyone to vote. Maybe that money could be diverted to three different projects, or as a family you only choose one cause to support each year. Through this process, your family would be more connected than in any previous years of the gift-buying merry-go-round, and your gift would go to a good cause. Maybe you should suggest a new family Christmas gift exchange this year!

When you collectively give as a family to the greatest passions of your family, you will be surprised how much more than twenty-five dollars each person gives because they're giving out of generosity and not out of obligation. Sharing our resources as a family is an ancient practice that could be reintegrated into the fabric of our families to bring us closer together again.

In this scenario, we learn about our families and contribute toward the causes our families care about. This could be the year that you exchange passions and give a gift to a need instead of just another want.

BIRTHDAY PRESENTS

I'll never forget my first car ride with Eugene Cho. He sat in the backseat, I sat in front, and the driver was Dave Gibbons, pastor of Newsong Church.[6]

When we started driving, Dave simply said, "The two of you need to know each other." And the conversation began. Eugene told me about a new organization he felt called to initiate in Seattle called One Day's Wages.[7]

He asked me, "What do you think is the most selfish day of the year? Our birthdays, right?" On our birthdays, we wake up, and everyone buys us something. Everything is focused on us this one day. Eugene was right in every way. That's probably why we all love our birthdays; some of us even tell everyone that our birthday is coming and throw a big party.

So, here's the question: if we don't need anything that day and everything is gifted to us, why wouldn't we give our earnings from that day to others? Specifically, Eugene's vision is to challenge others to give away one day's wages each year on their birthdays, with the goal of ending global poverty. On that day, we have excess. So on our birthdays, a day when we usually have more than enough, let's give away our excess. My instant response was to ask myself, *How much is one day of my wages?* I had never thought about this before my conversation with Eugene. On many trips overseas, I've heard aid workers quantify one day's wages for the average worker in a particular community, but this is not a term we often quantify in the United States. One day's wages is simply 0.4 percent of your annual salary.

Here's a rough guide:

ONE DAY'S WAGES CHART

	Annual Salary: $10,000	One Day's Wages: $40
	Annual Salary: $20,000	One Day's Wages: $80
	Annual Salary: $30,000	One Day's Wages: $120
	Annual Salary: $40,000	One Day's Wages: $160
	Annual Salary: $50,000	One Day's Wages: $200

	Annual Salary: $60,000	One Day's Wages: $240
	Annual Salary: $70,000	One Day's Wages: $280
	Annual Salary: $80,000	One Day's Wages: $320
	Annual Salary: $90,000	One Day's Wages: $360
	Annual Salary: $100,000	One Day's Wages: $400

Now for a brief moment, consider that over three billion people in the world live on less than $2.50 per day.[8] Looking at this simple chart brings our perspective of how rich we really are into great clarity.

The most powerful part of the story of Eugene Cho was the choice that he and his family made for the year before launching One Day's Wages. He felt a deep conviction about how he could approach others. When you ask people to give to your charity, others tend to critique your character, motivation, and system very quickly. He knew his character in asking would only be shown through his personal life story. Eugene asks others to give away one *day's* wages. He chose to give away one *year's* wages. Eugene said it succinctly, "We are not asking others to do something we are not willing to do ourselves."[9] In total, he chose to give away sixty-eight thousand dollars before he started his nonprofit. He continued to work for one year and gave away every dollar that he earned. This radical expression of voluntary suffering and excessive generosity is commendable and almost unfathomable.

Eugene also introduced to me two new terms that continually challenge my perspective on the desire of progress: downward mobility and upward mobility.[10] These are sociological terms that refer to a vertical shift in social-class distinction known as the Social Mobility Theory. Upward mobility, as you might expect, is when a person's social status moves higher. Downward mobility results in a lower position in that same societal system.[11]

Eugene shared that the greatest example of downward mobility is the story of Jesus: "Jesus ... gave up the glory of heaven to descend upon this world; he gave up total divinity to be consumed by flesh and bone and to simultaneously assume full humanity.... [T]hroughout his life, he owned nothing except the stuff he traveled with."[12]

Contrast that with the American story of constant desire for eternal upward mobility. Eugene stated: "We want to upgrade everything at every opportunity. We want the bestest, the fastest, the strongest, the mightiest, the largest, the mostest ... the list goes on and on.... Upward mobility never stops."[13]

When I think about all the situations in which presents play a role (birthdays, Christmas, Father's Day, Mother's Day, Valentine's Day), I always desire upward mobility. I want to acquire something that bumps up my social status. After our birthdays, for example, others will often ask us: "What did you get?" Our answer is usually bent toward securing our bump, however small, in social status. But what if at times we chose a downwardly mobile solution to position ourselves more humbly?

On our most selfish day of the year, let's all consider ways to lift up the great needs of others and knock down our selfish ambition. When we voluntarily choose the road of downward mobility to raise the social status of another human's potential, we gain status that is greater than cultural class, false importance, or economic success. Like Jesus, we gain status in a different sort of success matrix by becoming a living and breathing example of hope on earth.

A DIFFERENT REGISTRY

Cindy Simmons is a radio personality and star of "Cindy and Ray in the Morning" on Star 94 in Atlanta. She attended one of our gatherings in the city and shared with me how we could help her out with her upcoming wedding.

On her blog, Cindy explained further: "My fiancé Eric and I believe we already have everything we need to start our lives together. Why in the world would we need another toaster, blender, or towel? … However, we do believe in our hearts that what we really want and need is to be able to help others and if we can give that super fun feeling to someone else … that would be a pretty awesome thing!"[14]

So, they partnered with Wellspring Living to create a different kind of Target wedding registry. Wellspring Living[15] is a nonprofit organization that aids in the rehabilitation and restoration of women and girls who have been sexually abused or exploited. "We … wanted to be able to make a wedding registry 100% for the girls at Wellspring Living," Cindy continued. "We were able to have the girls actually go to Target, grab a registry gun and point away! They found tons of great items to make their new home feel like a home."[16]

Eric and Cindy realized that they didn't need more. They didn't even desire more. They already lived with more than enough, so they wanted to give to others in need. This story is a beautiful example of a couple who had already received enough gifts and wanted to give more to others. Their special day turned into less about their upward mobility and more about the needs that were addressed for others.

ENOUGH TALK

My parents now have nine grandchildren that fill our home every Christmas to celebrate the season. We quickly realized that none of our kids and definitely none of the adults needed any more presents, so my sisters came up with a new way to celebrate the day.

Every year each family brings our change jars to our special family gathering. We also bring catalogs we receive from charitable organizations like Compassion International[17], World Vision[18], Heifer International[19], Hope International[20], Samaritan's Purse[21], International Justice Mission[22], etc. We get together and dump all the change in the middle of the living room (each family usually adds in a few extra twenty-dollar bills). Then all the kids begin to organize the change roll by roll.

After we add up all the money, the grandkids then look through the catalogs and pick out what they want to buy for others across the world. Over the years, we've bought animals, started businesses, sent medical packages, and purchased English as a Second Language materials for those in need. Now, every family member looks forward to Christmas for a whole new reason.

This is an easy practice to do today. Dump out your change, count it up, and give it to an organization in great need. If you can add up at least fifty dollars in change, you can send it to Hope International; they will start a new business in the world, helping to lift someone out of poverty today. Now that is a gift worthy of giving.

[7]

ENOUGH
TRANSPORTATION

The ultimate measure of a man is not where he stands
in moments of comfort and convenience, but where
he stands at times of challenge and controversy.

—*Dr. Martin Luther King Jr., "On Being a Good Neighbor"*

As long as Andre can remember, she has known a deep calling to serve those in need of medical attention. Specifically, she wants to help meet the needs of vulnerable people who do not have access to medical care and can't afford all the treatments necessary. She served across the world in the slums of Nairobi, in a demobilized child soldier camp in southern Sudan, in southern parts of the state of Georgia with immigrant farm workers, and most recently in our city of Atlanta. Today, she works for Grady Memorial Hospital, widely known for its trauma and emergency services. Even more than that, Grady serves the community in diverse and powerful ways, bringing health care to the people that need it most in our city.

In addition, Andre has served in a neighborhood clinic as a physician assistant for more than five years, an experience that gives her an up-close picture of the daily lives of her regular patients. Much the way my relationship with Clarence helped me see my world in a new way, Andre's ongoing interactions with her patients continuously challenge her definitions of necessity and convenience. Let me give you an example.

Imagine you get paid eight dollars per hour working at a fast-food chain. The only way you get paid is to work. If you feel sick and stay home, you don't get paid. If you miss an eight-hour shift, you are not paid sixty-four dollars that day. Sixty-four dollars is one-twentieth of your income for the month. Let's say that you feel bad enough that you decide you need to go to the hospital to get checked out. Coughing, with a splitting headache, you walk five blocks to the bus station. You wait twenty minutes for a bus and ride it another thirty minutes to get to the bus stop nearest to the clinic. The clinic is still another two blocks away. In total, it took you at least one hour to make it to the clinic and two dollars and fifty cents to ride the bus one way. Next, you add your name to a rapidly growing list and hope they have time for yet another walk-in. You wait for two more hours to see a physician. After you see the doctor, you have a bill (thankfully built from a sliding scale based on income levels) for twenty-five dollars. The doctor recommends the two cheapest possible _____ for your illness, but the medicine still adds an additional twenty-five dollars to your bills for the day. It takes you another hour and another two dollars and fifty cents to return home. In total, the cost for the day is one hundred and nineteen dollars, and you spent more than four hours of time. That is now one-tenth of your monthly income. If you make eight dollars per hour and work forty hours per week, you make one thousand, two hundred and eighty dollars per month. On top of that, you didn't get any rest to treat your illness, and your chances of missing work the next day are extremely high.

Some slight variation of this story characterizes a large number of the patients Andre sees every day. Unlike many of her family-practice counterparts' experience, when a patient comes to see her, it is truly a necessity, and it's anything but convenient. Most of the patients she sees do not own or have access to what a large number of Americans see as everyday necessities. The way they live day-to-day life—and therefore, the way they see and interpret the world—is radically different than the way Andre would if it weren't for her patients.

In the Christian tradition, Lent is the forty-day period of the liturgical year from Ash Wednesday to Easter. The traditional purpose of Lent is to prepare the believer—through prayer, repentance, and self-denial—for the commemoration of the death and resurrection of Jesus. Andre and I have chosen to participate in Lent for many years, and more recently, we've chosen to give up something in order to help us meaningfully connect with the suffering of others.

As Andre interacted with her patients, she tried to imagine a way that she could walk in their shoes during Lent. She chose a voluntary act of personal suffering that would mirror the journey her patients took to see her. We live close enough to her work (about a mile and a half each way) that she chose to walk to work every day. A bus was not necessary. It was far enough that it was annoying and close enough to push through each day. If someone offered her a ride while she was walking, she would take it, but she would never ask for a ride. As it turned out, she walked in rain. She walked in ninety-degree heat. She walked on beautiful spring mornings and pollen-drifting afternoons. It didn't take her long to learn some important survival tips. She learned to wear running shoes and carry her work shoes. She learned to carry an umbrella at all times, not knowing what the weather would bring each day. She brought an extra outfit in her backpack in case of either rain or sweat from the walk. She also had to wake up earlier and made it home later than usual.

Along the way, she chose to pray for all her patients. As she walked, she thought through the people with whom she'd interacted the day before, and the list of people she knew were on the horizon for the day ahead. She chose not to use her phone on her walks so she could focus on the experiment she had chosen. When Andre chose to walk in the shoes of her patients, she gained a deeper patience for their stories and health concerns. She regained the "why" behind "what" she did every day. She gained a new sense of empathy for the fatigue of someone who was tired before they stepped onto the bus, the frustration of those who had already waited at the bus stop and in the waiting room and had to wait again in the examination room. She better understood the challenge that a referral to another office posed for someone without his or her own vehicle. And she began once again to see her job as not just a job, but also as a purpose.

It's hard to get into the minds of others, to truly understand the people we love. Sometimes we must physically change our environment before we can understand the space of others. To walk in the shoes of those we love, serve, or just want to understand is an act of empathy that will change you and transform the way you see their lives forever. It allows the story of our neighbor into our physical experience and our thinking. We will never fully understand how others live, but experiments like this can create a parallel experience that gives us a glimpse into their lives. And that intentionality and experience become a small part of our larger perspective. This kind of experience also plants seeds of mercy, empathy, and eventually community in our hearts.

The fact is that we need to let go of our convenience in order to gain a greater understanding of others' needs; we need to suffer with others, instead of simply pitying them. This kind of inconvenient practice creates a new paradigm that does more than help; it moves us toward deeper understanding. Helping others through voluntary suffering is a short-term experience that forces us to engage a long-term problem. Understanding others ultimately challenges us to live a life that is more inclusive of others.

Jean Vanier is the founder of the L'Arche Community[1] for the mentally handicapped and their helpers. Jean chose to live in a community with several people who are mentally handicapped. In his book *Community and Growth* he talked about what he learned while living in solidarity with his friends, writing that "freedom doesn't grow in the abstract; it grows in a particular soil with particular people. Inner growth is only possible when we commit ourselves with and to others. We all have to pass through a certain death and time of grief when we make choices and become rooted."[2] He acknowledged that the journey to engage in the suffering of others is not an easy choice, but he also said that it is the place where we grow the most.

The forty days of Lent painted a vivid mental picture for Andre that will stick with her. Because she chose the inconvenient route, she now has a deeper understanding of what necessity means in the lives of the people she serves. Bob Dylan wrote the following words in a song called "Brownsville Girl": "Strange how people who suffer together have stronger connections than people who are most content."[3] He went on to observe, "People don't do what they believe in, they just do what's most convenient, then they repent."[4]

That line unsettles me every time I hear it. Convenience is such an important value in much of American society that we no longer recognize it as optional. It has become a necessity. On a daily basis, I make myriad decisions that fall on what I now recognize as the continuum of necessity and convenience. Convenience usually drives how I determine what is necessary. Understanding the difference between convenience and necessity, and how they control our decisions, plays a significant role in determining how we live. Letting go of convenience will never be an easy choice, but it may be the most significant choice for you and others. Choosing to do something significant in life usually requires us to sacrifice our personal convenience, but the results can be life changing for ourselves and those around us.

- *Visual Moment*
  Watch Andre's story: www.moreorlessbook.com/#videos

THIS-OMETER AND THAT-BURATOR

Lesley Carter lives just down the street from our house and is an integral part of our community in endless ways. One summer, her car broke down at one of the most inconvenient places you could imagine—in the middle of one of the busiest roads of Atlanta, a road known for its horrendous traffic. Her car died, and she couldn't even get it to the side of the road. After surviving the initial event, Lesley recounted the continuing nightmare: "After getting it towed from one garage to another, after having circular conversations with mechanics about this-ometer and that-burator, it became clear that getting my car up and running again would cost upwards of twelve hundred dollars—money that I didn't have."

So she had two options:

Option #1: She could put the twelve hundred dollars on credit and pay it off over the next six months or longer, adding another item to her list of monthly transportation expenses that already included gas, insurance, maintenance, and the car payments she still made. All this included the likely probability that her car would require other expensive repairs down the road.

Option #2: Lesley could upgrade to a newer vehicle, saving the repair expenses but adding a new car loan to her pile of debt.

She wasn't particularly excited about either of those options, but what choice did she have? She needed a car. Or did she need a car? In her own words:

> This is Atlanta, not New York. You can't just hop on the subway at the next corner and get where you want to go. Atlanta is a driving city, and a car is necessary to survival. Except … well, is it? As I turned that question over in my head, I began to wonder just how much truth was in the notion that having a car was an absolute imperative in a city like Atlanta. It's true; we don't have a slick and extensive public transit system. But we do have one (MARTA). True, it's a pain to stand outside waiting for a bus. But does pain equal impossible?[5]

As she pondered those questions, she began to sketch the outlines of an Enough Experiment:

Option #3: "Ditch the junk heap and don't replace it. Rely exclusively on public transportation and the occasional ride from a friend. See if it works—and if so, for how long?"

That was more than three years ago:

And here I am, still in Atlanta and still car-less. I have braved every kind of weather and have trudged through many a diverse terrain—sometimes in heels. I've learned to edge heels out of my everyday wardrobe. I've also learned that buses tend to run five to fifteen minutes behind schedule, that trains could use more handles and poles for the standing people to hold onto, and that the umbrella that fits in your bag is really only going to keep the top of your head dry. I've even learned how to predict whether a man's going to give up his seat to a lady based on how nicely he's dressed. Clue: the more expensive the shoes, the less likely he is to stand in them for your sake.[6]

More than anything, Lesley learned how much the convenience of owning a car cost her every month—both in terms of money and stress. In contrast to those tensions, she experienced the high value of her close friendships: "Sometimes you've just got to get somewhere quickly, and at those times the friend that will give you a lift begins to look like Mother Teresa. But that, of course, comes with the price of swallowing all of your I'm-doing-this-on-my-own pride long enough to ask for help."[7]

The question is simple: is a car a necessity for Lesley? She said:

When it comes down to it, people often say "necessary" when what they really mean is "convenient."

And I'll give them that; it's incredibly convenient to own a car. It's inconvenient to make dinner plans and have to leave an hour ahead of time to catch the right buses. It's inconvenient to carry a heavy coat well into the spring because you know you'll be standing outside before the temperature breaks out of the fifties. It's a nightmare to run into an unexpected rainstorm. It's uncomfortable to be jammed into a small space with people you don't know. It's stressful to hop off the bus and wander through unfamiliar and maybe unscrubbed areas of town on foot, trying to look like you're not lost. It's unsettling sometimes to be in such close proximity to the homeless.[8]

Many of us pay a lot of money for convenience. Too often my view of convenience determines what I think is necessity. Lesley's decision to go carless may not be convenient while she's waiting at the bus stop, but it paid off when she looked for a new job. She applied for a job with a local clean-air organization that felt like a perfect fit for her skills and expertise. Her transportation lifestyle decisions helped to tip the scale in her favor and secured her dream job with the company.

In retrospect, Leslie shared some profound thoughts with me about the experiment:

We run into trouble when we stop recognizing our conveniences and allow them to masquerade as essentials. Most of them are not essential at all. It's telling that when you look up *convenience* in a thesaurus, you find *luxury* and *extravagance* listed among its synonyms. In a driving city, the car-less life is a complicated one. But it's not necessarily a deprived one.[9]

I'm not suggesting that everybody go out and sell their car and ride the bus for the rest of their lives just because Lesley had a significant experience using mass transportation. I understand that most people in America don't actually have a mass transportation option to move them from one place to another. For most of the people reading this book, this experiment is not a viable option. Lesley's real-life experience, however, shows that we probably have other examples of conveniences in our lives that masquerade as necessities. And sometimes those "necessities" inconvenience our lives more than we realize.

NECESSARY CONVENIENCE

During Lent one year I decided to give up coffee. This may not seem significant to some of you, but my daily life depends on drinking a minimum of one cup of fully caffeinated coffee every morning. My sister likes to call it an addiction, probably because it is one, albeit a legal and socially acceptable addiction.

So for forty days, I would stop drinking coffee. I know what you are thinking. Andre's Lent choice was a much more significant act of voluntary suffering than mine. You're right, but that doesn't mean refraining from coffee for forty days was easy. When you've consumed a minimum of one cup (and let's be honest, it was often three or four cups) of coffee every morning for more than fourteen years, and then you quit instantly, *it hurts*. For the first three weeks I went without coffee I had a constant headache, and as a result, those were the least creative forty days of my life. I made it, and I hated it. Sometimes the things that truly hurt are the best things for us. This kind of pain is never convenient, but it may be a necessary evil that gives us a greater understanding and appreciation for the taste of things that are good.

After forty days, I started drinking coffee again. I loved it too much to live without it. However, my love affair with coffee and all of the ways I can get it into my mug forces me to think about convenience. An entire industry has been built around the quality of coffee, the value of coffee, and how we drink our coffee—all of which is built around convenience.

There are myriad ways to get and make your coffee, including instant, pre-ground, pre-ground and pre-separated, whole bean (in a variety of flavors), French Press, pour-over brewing process, your local coffee shop—and of course, you can drive through Starbucks. Each of these options comes with a varying level of convenience.

Once the coffee is brewed, you have many options for how you drink your coffee. You can drink from a ceramic coffee mug, reusable travel mug, glass mug, plastic mug, paper cup, or a Styrofoam cup, and some of these come with a coffee sleeve, so we don't burn our fingers in the process. However you want your morning jolt, the coffee industry offers multiple options to serve your wants, conveniently.

By now, you may be thinking, *This is nice, Jeff, but what does it have to do with transportation?*

Coffee is a microstory of how convenience drives our commerce and how we make choices based on those conveniences. Most broadly adopted innovations today increase convenience, resulting in consumers integrating that innovation into our lives moving forward. Isn't it true that we want every aspect of life to be as easy and accessible as possible? We pay an extra three dollars for a "convenience fee" at ATMs that are not associated with our bank. We pay parking attendants a fee to conveniently park our car. We pay twelve dollars per month to conveniently record all of our favorite TV shows, so we can watch them when we want via TiVo or another DVR. When in doubt, we choose convenience as a necessity in our lives, and convenience now determines what we believe is necessary.

The Pew Research Center embarked on an eye-opening study that gives a remarkable snapshot of what we determine is necessary. The underlying question was simple: what would be on your list of things you can't live without? Eighty-eight percent of the people researched said they couldn't live without a car. Sixty-six percent needed a clothes dryer. Forty-seven percent couldn't live without a microwave. Fifty percent needed a home computer. Forty-nine percent needed a cell phone.[10] The list highlights many more objects that we all claim are necessities in our lives.

As I reviewed this research, I admit that I also felt that I *needed* all of the items listed. They are necessary in my life of convenience. The majority of these I barely had to work to own. I had access to these items or already owned them by the time I showed up for my first day of college. At age eighteen, I enjoyed food, shelter, and clothing, but also I embarked on four extra years of education with all the conveniences of modern-day American life. Since that time, I have upgraded nearly all of these "necessities" in one way or another. Some of these possessions I've upgraded multiple times. I started with the entry-level product and upgraded along the way to increase my convenience and social status.

The question is: do we need to reconsider what is essential versus what is a convenience? How can we step back and challenge our operational standards so that we can honestly rethink this question? What makes life easier for us but may not be essential to our lives? When we reimagine this as a continuum, we live differently. But we don't just do this to save money or for the sake of a changed perspective.

The conveniences that we increasingly convince ourselves are necessary for happy or successful life also separate us from those who do not have them. The more layers of convenience we add to our lives, the more space we create between us and those desperately working day to day to survive. As Lesley discovered riding the bus, convenience also tends to separate us, period. The more self-sufficient we are, the less we need others. The less we need others, the less likely we are to form the bonds of true community. Convenience enhances self-reliance, increases ease, and ironically, separates us from real relationships with people who have real needs.

My sister Joanna chose a different transportation path than Lesley. A few years ago, she and her husband downsized from a minivan to a five-passenger vehicle. Trying to be more economical and environmental, it seemed like a good decision. After a short time, however, they realized that it also affected their options for community building. When the car is already full, it's hard to invite a friend home from church. It became inconvenient for her kids to do things with their friends. Joanna also volunteers for her church's English as a Second Language program, where all of the students are recent immigrants to the United States. Very few of them have vehicles or a driver's license, and they often need rides to class, doctor's appointments, and immigration offices—and often the entire family needs to attend. Joanna's five-passenger vehicle was never large enough. With their income, she and her husband could afford a bigger vehicle, so they decided to use their excess to purchase a vehicle that allowed them to serve others and foster relationships.

Joanna explained, "Every week, I pick up a Burmese family of five to bring to ESL class. At first, it was frustratingly inconvenient. It took more time, and I had less flexibility in terms of what time I could get to class to set up and be prepared. Over time, however, I realized that those twenty minutes in the car every week had formed a friendship that I treasure far more than having a few extra minutes of prep time. Christmas Eve this year, fifty Burmese refugees stood outside my front door, singing Christmas carols in Karenni (their first language) to my family. It was the best gift I received this year."[11]

Not every choice to use our excess for good forces us to downsize. Most choices, however, do require thought and intentionality. *What is important to me? How do I utilize my stuff in a way that supports my beliefs? Is convenience more important than community? Who is important to me and how does that affect my daily choices?* These are the questions that can change our excess stuff into tools to use for good.

ENOUGH TALK

When was the last time you carpooled? I don't just mean sharing a ride with one other person, I mean practicing the inconvenience of carpooling in community?

Remember the idea of the "church bus" years ago? There was a driver who would get in a van and go pick up kids and bring them to church. What if you and your friends practiced this idea for one week? I know what you are thinking—you don't have a bus.

Choose a driver for the week. I will assume that the driver has room in their car for at least four others. That driver (I suggest it be you, since you are reading this book) commits to picking up four other friends, wherever they live, and taking them to wherever they are going, and of course dropping them off at the end of the day. Practice this for one evening, for one weekend, or even for a week. If you do this experiment multiple times, I suggest changing the order of pickups and drop-offs each time. You might have some of the best conversations with your friends while experiencing this slightly inconvenient practice together.

[8]

ENOUGH TIME

Happiness is not a matter of intensity but of
balance and order and rhythm and harmony.

—*Thomas Merton*

It was my freshman year at Spring Arbor University in Michigan. School rules required all students to attend an infamous weekend retreat at Cedar Bend.[1] Cedar Bend is a farm in northern Michigan designed to take guests back in time. Imagine turning off the highway and winding up in the world of Laura Ingalls Wilder and *Little House on the Prairie*. The main farmhouse features wood-burning stoves for heat and food, kerosene lamps for light, and handmade benches sure to give you a splinter if you sit just right.

Obviously, Cedar Bend lacks the tools of modern technology. There are no clocks, no watches, no laptops, no music devices, no Internet, no electricity, and no phones allowed. Just the land and whatever can be taken from the land for sustenance and enjoyment. All food is taken from the land, including vegetables, milk, cheese (churned from milk), and chickens, which must be killed and plucked to prepare for dinner. The most commonly asked question upon return from dinner preparation: "Who chopped the chicken's head off?" Cedar Bend inspired the best and most-often-repeated stories while simultaneously stirring up the most fear.

For two nights of the designed experience we stayed in the farmhouse and slept well with our sleeping bags sitting on roughly carved bunk beds or snuggled up next to one of the wood-burning fires. We drank hot chocolate and coffee from those blue mugs with speckles of black paint on them that always get too hot in your hands. We sang songs with the one person that brought a guitar. Some huddled around a lamp to play a game of euchre[2] (the card game of choice for anyone who grew up in Michigan) for a couple hours and ate popcorn popped over the stove. It was peaceful. We experienced some of the goodness of the early form of American life in which family was still valued and small innovations of convenience were few. Those two nights felt like communal living in an Amish farmhouse with some great friends.

After two nights, we took off on our "pilgrimage."

When the sun rose, we began walking. Organizers gave each team of twelve a large wooden box about four feet long, two feet wide, and two feet tall. In the box were a couple of rain tarps, rope, matches, flour, plates, forks, mugs, two pots, salt and pepper, and cheese (if the caretaker at the farm felt generous). Outside of the box, they provided two jerricans of water, each holding five gallons. Whatever you brought for the weekend, you must carry on your back. The four guys in the group who lost the quick rock, paper, scissors competition usually carried the box and the water.

Then we walked for what seemed like ages out into the middle of nowhere, with no buildings or signs of human life in sight.

When we finally arrived at our destination, marked on the maps, we began to fashion our temporary outpost. Two tasks consumed the day: constructing a shelter and building a fire. The fire was the easier option, assuming the wood was dry. We gathered leaves and twigs and placed a stack of wood large enough to last the day and night. It was important to store up enough wood to last us the night because we would count on it to cook food and keep us warm that evening. Let me remind you, this was fall in northern Michigan. Not only was it bound to get cold at night, but in the back of everyone's minds were the Cedar Bend stories containing the S word: *snow*.

Next, we moved to the tarps to build something to sleep under for the night. It was a life exercise in group dynamics. Everyone had an opinion, but we ultimately landed on a design and built the structure combining the rope, tarps, and nearby trees.

We spent whatever was left of the day working the land, digging up vegetables, and weeding the garden for the group coming the next week. We also cooked lunch and prepared for dinner by trying to make dumplings out of the flour. The food never turned out exactly how anyone intended, and we ate undercooked or burned potatoes and pitiful mush that we called dumplings. Before long, the team of twelve sat around the fire, some of us lying on our backs, staring at the darkness in every direction and the brightness of the stars. Inevitably, someone started the scary stories, and eventually everyone fell asleep.

I experienced Cedar Bend twice more as an assistant to the professor. Once, when the students fell asleep, the professor looked over at me and said, "What time do you think it is?" We made our guesses, then the professor pulled a watch out of his bag. Both times, the entire group was deep in sleep, a couple of students snoring rhythmically, between seven and eight o'clock. These were the same college students that were normally up until two in the morning, causing a ruckus on campus. One day of hard work wiped out these students as soon as the sun set.

Perhaps you've experienced something similar on a camping trip with family or friends. The combination of experiencing fresh air and sun, doing hard physical work, and disconnecting from technology leaves us exhausted soon after the sun goes down. I've also discovered that sometimes simply disconnecting from time-telling devices that tell us how much time we have and what we need to do with that time drastically affects us as well. The day we disconnect from technology, we become suddenly exhausted. When time is hard to quantify, our bodies instinctively speak to us about needing more rest. Meanwhile, on a day-to-day basis, there never seem to be enough minutes in the day for everything we need to do.

There is never enough time. We go to bed every night with a to-do list longer than is possible to complete the next day. We all balance our time between family, friends, clubs, associations, church, study groups, prayer, reading, the gym, meals, our kids' activities and sports, volunteering, and vacations. Simultaneously, we feel the need to document our lives through social media for whomever we're not appeasing with our time, so they can see that we're doing something significant with the time we're not spending with them. Meanwhile, we feel like we're not spending adequate time in any one of the categories on the list.

When we lament this sense of failure to a friend, he or she gently admonishes us, saying that our lives are out of balance. So we try to move the weights around on our scale to see if we can ease up the pain and live healthier lives. We pledge to get back to the basics. We plan out our week and try to be more intentional about spending time in each of these categories. Then we get to the end of the week and find we weren't able to stick to the schedule because fifty things that weren't in the plan came up out of nowhere—those things that are not just urgent but also important.

William Penn said, "Time is what we want most, but what we use worst." So we stay up late into the night trying to catch up and wake up early trying to catch up. We rob Peter of time to try to pay off Paul. Time continues to tick away. We negotiate with our families to try to appease everyone who we say we care most about. When we are with one person we are thinking about another. Then we get tired. We feel sick. We are not happy. Our spouse is not happy. Our friends become acquaintances. Everyone feels shorted of our time in some way. And they are right. We have failed. We can't do it all.

In her book *The Happiness Project*, Gretchen Rubin reminded us how to think about this very issue: "When I find myself focusing overmuch on the anticipated future happiness of arriving at a certain goal, I remind myself to 'Enjoy now.' If I can enjoy the present, I don't need to count on the happiness that is (or isn't) waiting for me in the future."[3]

In a book about using our excess for good, why did I include a chapter about time? We don't have excess time; if anything we never have enough. If Benjamin Franklin's famous phrase "Time is money" is true, then we often feel impoverished. Yet, as many books, speakers, and experts have reminded me over the years, we all have exactly the same number of hours in every day. The difference comes in how we choose to use them. In order to use our excess for good, it is crucial to have the time in order to *do good*. In order to define "what is enough" for me in any area of my life, I need to take the time to evaluate where I am and where I want to be. Most of the world's major religions have some form of The Golden Rule in their teachings: do unto others as you would have them do unto you. We give lip service to the idea that people are supremely important. But what does our use of time say is important?

BUSY IS THE NEW FINE

Recently I started to recognize a pattern emerging in my daily polite interactions:

> Me: "Hey, Joe! Good to see you. How are you?"
> Joe: "Busy. Been a crazy month. How are you?"
> Me: "Busy. A lot is happening right now."

Barista: "Good morning! How are you today?"

Me: "Busy. How are you?"

Barista: "It's been a busy morning!"

Notice a pattern here? There was a time, not so long ago, when the polite answer to the question "How are you?" was, "Fine." It seems that *busy* is the new fine. We look at one another with that shake of the head, sideways smirk, and glossy eyes, proclaiming our busyness. This shared response succinctly identifies a recent cultural shift: we now determine the significance of a person by how busy they are. Somehow, busy has become better than fine. It seems especially highlighted since the economic downturn. Busy shows that we still have a job and things to do, which is a positive answer amidst the endlessly looping, negative news cycle.

The problem is this: busy is not better than fine. Just because I'm busy does not mean I'm fine. And when it comes right down to it, often busy means that I'm not fine at all. What we're really saying with one simple word is, "I can't keep up with everything in my life. I actually can't keep up with any of the things in my life. But that makes me important, doesn't it?"

Does anyone else feel like they've become a professional juggler? At any given time I am juggling twenty balls above my head. I catch one in my hand and with as much momentum as possible I throw it right back up. The ball goes high enough to give me time to catch and release the other nineteen balls before I have to catch the first ball just before it hits the ground. But the balls keep getting closer and closer to the floor, and before you know it, one hits the ground, and then they all hit the ground. Even a professional juggler can't keep up with all the juggling in our lives. There are too many balls in the air.

Often the first ball we drop is our relationships. Being "busy" quickly becomes a barrier or excuse in the way of true community. I am busy, and many of my friends know that I am busy. When the only answer I ever give them in response to the question "How are you?" is, "Busy," this communicates that I don't have time for them. When I constantly say, "I'm busy," I communicate to others that "I don't need you right now." Most of our friends pick up this subtle message and stay away.

What we often realize too late is that our "busy" answer is actually a choice not to engage in community. We choose to do other stuff over hanging out with our friends. If I continue to tell myself the lie that busy is good, I slowly enter into more of an isolated and a self-centered existence.

● *Visual Moment*
Watch a reflection on our busy world:
www.moreorlessbook.com/#videos

DO YOU HAVE WANDERING EYES?

Let me paint you a picture. You attend a social gathering of some kind, and there are twenty-five people in the room. You connect with a friend, and the conversation is going great. You're catching up beyond just the surface niceties. You've just begun to share something that you know your friend would love to hear when a new group of people enters the room. Your friend's eyes wander to the new group, and you watch him both physically and mentally check out. How do you feel?

A moment before, you felt important and connected to this person. Suddenly you feel like you've moved down a couple of notches on the social-status totem pole. I've been the recipient of the wandering eyes before, but I've also been the person with wandering eyes—as I'm sure you have too. But I don't want to be that person anymore.

Sometimes people are truly busy and need to focus on the task at hand. But if we are too busy to engage in relationships, we face a larger problem. When I respond and tell you I am too busy, too often I actually need your help. Often in those times when we most need a deep relationship, instead of pursuing that relationship, we embrace our task list and avoid the comfort and support that true friendship can offer. And the result of being extra busy, ironically, is loneliness and depression.

If you are one of the people who isn't caught up in the "busy cycle," please reach out to those who are caught in it. We need your example. We need your gentle insistence that community *is* good. That friendship *is* golden. That the things that need to get done can wait. And that you will love us no matter how much or how little we accomplish on our checklist. Most of all, we need you to teach us and remind us how to be fully present.

What does it mean to be present?

Presence is the gift my dad gave me when he attended every sports game I played, even when his schedule was busy. Presence is the friend who just sits next to you during a family funeral and doesn't say a word. Presence is picking up the phone every time your close friend calls rather than letting it go to voice mail … *again*. Presence is not fast, big, or cheap. You cannot replace presence with someone or something else. Presence is an essential element that we all need and desire in our deepest relationships. It's unspoken. It's true. It's the greatest encouragement anyone can ever receive or give. Presence is a physical expression of love in the midst of a culture that never stops—it is to stop and be with someone that matters.

Andre and our friend Allison Dudley talked at length about this one evening. It seems that the most interesting person in the room, and the person we often compete with for attention, isn't a person at all—it's a cell phone. How often have you been at a restaurant with friends and you see everyone looking down at their phones and updating the world on what they're doing, as if it were that important. Or even in our homes, we gather for a fun night of games, and yet the phones are a constant distraction.

As they talked, Andre and Allison imagined an intentional experiment to combat this problem. They decided to proactively change the environment of our homes by placing a basket next to the front door and then inviting guests to place their mobile devices inside for the duration of their stay. Andre wrote about her intentions with this basket. "Please understand, this is in no way meant to be rude or even problematic; it is solely meant for you and me to purposefully engage in meaningful conversation. A place to feel safe with no interruptions. No side glances down to my phone to see that text. No phone calls that can somehow put a damper on the important issue at hand. Equally important, no using the device to disengage in moments of silence in the conversation." Allison added one small touch to the basket that communicates so clearly their intention and challenge. On the front of the basket she wrote these words: "Be with the ones that are here."

I want to be able to give time freely to the person standing in front of me. I want to do less searching and contribute more to the present moment. I want to be present with my family, with my friends, at work, and in my conversations. I want to be known as a person who is fully here, fully present. But this kind of presence begins by choosing to be less busy.

THE TIME INDICATOR

The way I choose to use my time is as much an indicator of who I am as the way I choose to spend my money. Time is money in the sense that it is a commodity we can give that offers value to people or things. As I've thought through the way that time influences my life, I've realized several things.

1. Those with Whom You Spend Your Time Will Strongly Influence What You Desire.

When I spend most of my time with people who have a greater amount of wealth or influence than I have, my desires begin to

shift to match the values of that person. When I'm around someone who enjoys a greater cultural position than I do, I desire to
become more financially successful. Conversely, when I spend the
majority of my time with people who have less money or influence, my posture shifts dramatically. I begin to simplify the things
I wear, the place I live, the car I drive, and where I eat my next
meal. As a result, I try to simplify the view I have of myself in
the context of the greater world. Whether we realize it or not, the
people with whom we choose to spend our time play a significant
role in the desires of our hearts.

Question: with whom are you spending your time, and how
do those people influence what you want?

2. The Way You Spend Your Excess Time Shows What You Really Want.

What do you spend your free time doing, and why? How often do
you stop to think about the way that you spend your time? What
does that show you about what you really desire or who you hope
to become?

Have you ever heard of the term *daylighting*?[4] For you, daylighting might be a side project or personal hobby that you hope
to make into a lifestyle someday, or perhaps it's simply working a
second job while keeping your primary job. Whatever you call it,
there's a good chance you've done this in some form or fashion.
You do one thing to pay the bills, while your passion waits in the

wings for your undivided attention. Often our free time is consumed with the desires of our calling. Our quest is to find a way to make more of our time dedicated to the pursuit of these dreams.

Question: how do you make time for the things you are passionate about?

3. The More Time You Give to Everything, the Less Focused You Are on What Matters.

Young leaders today are often referred to as the slash/slash generation. Nisha Gupta, in a piece for *Hudson/Houston*, explained it more fully:

> We are … a group of people that define ourselves
> not by a single occupation, but by the diversity of
> our experiences, passions and networks. Instead of
> carving out an upward trajectory life path within
> one career, we seek to gather as many experiences
> as possible to contribute to our multi-faceted
> lifestyle. It's more about creating a lifestyle than a
> life path. And the more multi-faceted the better.[5]

As interesting as this path might be, the pursuit of everything can result in a profession of nothing. Life experience gives us all great stories to share over a drink with new friends, but it can also result in exhaustion, loneliness, and the search for deeper meaning.

We can't do everything; we need to understand our own limitations and pursue our true purpose. When we try doing everything, we're probably not doing any one thing very well.

GROUNDED

Gisele Nelson was our first employee at Plywood People, and she contributes to our projects in every way imaginable. She is one of those people who makes everything and everyone around her better, and she gets everything done. She prides herself on having fewer than fifteen emails in her inbox at all times, sometimes to a fault, which results in her working too much.

One day she realized that her commitment to doing too much resulted in personal unhappiness. Gisele is an introvert who allowed busyness to overtake her life.

"I was busy all day long and every night," she shared. "I love time alone, it's how I recharge, but the expectations I put on myself in order to cater to the people in my life that I love, a job I'm passionate about, and a church I believe in, left me overwhelmed and extremely unhappy."[6]

She decided to make a drastic decision of personal discipline, to regain presence in her life, relationships, and quality of work. "So I grounded myself," she said.

Remember when your parents grounded you? It was usually a kind of punishment for disobeying them. They forced you to stay home, and you weren't allowed to play with your friends. Gisele intentionally chose a self-induced grounding to concentrate on slowing down her life. Life had become a consumption pattern, and it moved too fast to observe, critique, and discern. Gisele lives with intention, and she focuses with her friends. She works hard and gives every task 100 percent of her attention. But things had started to move out of sync with her best rhythm of life, and she decided she wanted to approach life differently.

Gisele created a set of guidelines for her grounding experience, simple parameters to accomplish her very own Enough Experiment. Her grounding consisted of only going out one night a week, eating healthy meals at home, exercising, and going to bed early. "I knew unless I made a real commitment to it, I would never actually make any changes. I prioritized my spirituality, and I learned some really valuable lessons along the way," she said.[7]

Gisele learned five things from being grounded that she hopes to integrate into the balance of her life moving forward:

1. Discipline follows discipline. When we become disciplined in one area of our lives, discipline in other areas follow. Making a choice to celebrate the practice of self-discipline sets a standard of wisdom for other actions in our lives, and a progression of lifestyle emerges that reflects greater thought and practice. Making one careful choice often leads to another.

2. When we stop being busy, we start being honest. When we choose to live in solitude, this practice reveals anxieties that are often overshadowed by busyness. Taking time for silence forces us to confront our fears, unhealthy behaviors, and deepest sins. When we stay busy, we quickly lose the practice of self-evaluation. We become a blur to the internal need for growth and simply move on to the next activity. Being grounded is a time to intentionally pursue self-actualization and personal growth.

3. Solitude is not selfish. At times, in order to gain focus in life, we need to make drastic changes that others might not understand. Just because someone else doesn't understand our priorities does not mean that those things shouldn't be prioritized. If the busyness of your life includes a large number of people, it's natural for some of them to take your choice for solitude personally. Choosing solitude is a choice to feed your soul, mind, and emotions as much as literal food and water are necessary for your physical health. It's helpful to be prepared to respond to questions from others.

4. Intentionality makes relationships better. Learning the discipline of solitude causes intentionality in relationships. If time with others is carefully given, our time together is intentional, and we want every minute to count.

5. Quitting (for a little while) makes work better. No matter how many tasks pull for our attention, sometimes it's better to put them away instead of just trudging through. Taking a break from tasks may be good. When I come back to them later, I'll attack the tasks with better efficiency, vision, and fervor.

Gisele's grounding of herself taught me an important lesson. There are two ways to look at time: you can define your time, or you can let others define time for you. If you want to determine how to use your time and what you will accomplish with it, then you have to proactively claim it. The only way to change your dilemma of time is to deliberately choose to live with a new clock.

ENOUGH TALK

Now is as good a time as any to stop being busy. Ground yourself for a day. Say no to all commitments, meetings, activities, and people. Find a place to go where you don't know anyone. Put away your watch, smart phone, and computer. Breathe deeply. Drink in some natural beauty. Spend a day being instead of doing.

Bring a blank journal, and write about whatever comes to your mind. Take a slow walk. Take a long run. Go somewhere beautiful in your area that you always intended to see but never got around to seeing. Ground yourself, and see how you feel about time—during and after.

ENOUGH ACCESS

I try to give to the poor people for love what
the rich could get for money. No, I wouldn't
touch a leper for a thousand pounds; yet I
willingly cure him for the love of God.

—*Mother Teresa*

We arrived in Nashville to visit our friends and their new baby. Eric and Melissa have such an amazing intentionality about how they live. Maybe you have friends like this, ones who choose to think before doing. They are dreamers who are wise in choosing what dreams to chase and how to chase them. They also love to create and live a good story.

We stayed in Nashville just one night on our way to Michigan to visit family, and their home and company offered a welcome respite from traveling with our one-year-old. They hired a babysitter for the night so the four of us could go out on a hot double date and catch up on life. Andre, Melissa, and I had no idea what our plans were for the evening, but Eric had a plan. We were going to see U2. Bono and the crew were in town for a show, and the city was about to explode.

There was just one problem: *we didn't have tickets.*

Eric, however, seemed confident. The Vanderbilt University football stadium was the venue for the concert, and apparently he knew of a parking deck that sat parallel with the stadium. For football games at Vanderbilt, students lined the second, third, and fourth levels of the deck, hanging over the side to watch the games. So Eric planned to watch the concert from the same spot as the hipsters do for every football game. All of a sudden we were fifteen years old again and boldly defying the traditional forms of access. Who needs a ticket when you can watch U2 play for free? We're smarter than the man. So we were all in, but our thirty-year-old minds secretly assumed that this utopian idea surely wouldn't work.

We parked the car about two miles away from the stadium (as a few other people planned on attending this concert as well). The air tingled with excitement. The combination of the anticipation and crowds of people put an extra bounce in our steps. We made it to the stadium and followed Eric's lead to the parking deck. It was a classic parking deck in that it was five stories high and nothing spectacular. A four-foot-high concrete barricade surrounded each level, making it just high enough to keep people in and low enough to allow one to see over the edge. So we walked directly up to the fourth floor without a hitch and joined about thirty other people standing on the deck who had the same devious plan. We were in. We could see the humongous stage that defined the U2

Global Tour that year. We had a perfect view of the big screen. Somehow, miraculously, we got access.

As the pre-show music started to get louder in the stadium, we looked over the edge at something directly below our deck. The entire band, including The Edge and Bono, walked right below our position on their way inside the stadium and onto the stage to rock the sold-out crowd.

Needless to say, Eric was the hero of the night. The band rocked, the lights pulsed, and we jumped up and down, going crazy for about six songs. That's when security showed up. It was kind of like getting to eat only half a cupcake, but it was better than nothing at all.

Something about being given access feels good. It lifts your spirit. It feels like a once-in-a-lifetime opportunity. *All Access.* It's the badge everyone wants to wear. You feel important, more important than others. It's the badge that says, "Those tape lines are for the rest of you, but not for me. Door? What door? This one that I can open and walk through?"

One week prior to our mini-adventure, a bunch of my friends convened in Denver to watch another U2 concert with a special backstage pass that allowed them to watch the concert from the pit, literally inside and surrounded by the staging. *Their tickets were free.* They enjoyed every luxury. One week later, I stood on my tiptoes just trying to get a glimpse of the screen. Our view was not exclusive. Our access was sneaky, and we caught a glimpse of something spectacular.

Access creates a strong contrast in our society. We either are granted access, or we are not. You're in or you're out. The danger is that sometimes we end up selling our souls for the right kind of access.

YES OR NO

Have you ever stopped to think about the most powerful words in any language? I believe the most powerful words are *yes* and *no*.

I recently watched an interview with Tom Cruise on *Inside The Actors Studio*[1], and the host asked him, "What is your favorite word in the dictionary?" Tom quickly answered, "Yes." His least favorite word? "No."

We love people who say yes to us. And we constantly say yes to others. Ironically, the more we say yes, the less we control or enjoy. The more we say no, the fewer commitments we guarantee. But often we're afraid of saying no. We want to please others so we say yes. Or too often we don't answer either way. We don't express an opinion, which results in poor decisions that aren't clear to anyone. When we fail to be decisive about our priorities, others can take advantage of us through our yesses and nos.

Poet Carl Sandburg wrote that time should be determined by our desires, not the desires of others. "Time is the coin of your life," Sandburg once said. "It is the only coin you have, and only you can determine how it will be spent. Be careful lest you let other people spend it for you." The two most powerful words in the dictionary are *yes* and *no*. We must learn to use these words purposefully for the things in our lives that matter most.

UNDERSTAND LIMITATIONS

As a young business owner, I wanted to make sure our venture would succeed. My greatest priority financially was earning enough money to cover the business expenses and still pay myself. My business method became "Take Any Project Offered," and I would commit to the impossible to secure the greatest opportunity. Inevitably, some projects did not get completed as promised, forcing me to apologize for the results. Over time, I couldn't keep up with time lines, the budget was never enough, and when I tried to do too many projects at once, the quality of all of them began to suffer. I quickly realized that I couldn't take on every project. I started to recognize my limitations and discovered the fact that I'm not designed to do everything. I am designed to carry out a finite number of projects and initiatives. Anything that I commit to that goes beyond my limitations will result in an inadequate result.

As Ruth Haley Barton so eloquently put it,

> Living within our limits means living within the finiteness of who we are as individuals and as a community—the limits of time and space, the limits of our physical, emotional, relational and spiritual capacities, the limits of our stage of life … and the limits of the calling that God has given. It means doing this and not that. It means doing this much and not more.

> When we refuse to live within our limits ... we
> wear out ourselves and those who lead with us....
> We compromise our effectiveness at doing the
> things we have been called to do. To live within
> our limits is to live humbly as the creature and
> not the Creator. Only God is infinite; the rest of
> us need to be very clear about what we are to be
> about in any given moment and say no to every-
> thing else.[2]

Many of us have Superman ambitions, wishing we could do
more than is humanly possible, but in the end we must realize
that there is only One possessing greater-than-human abilities. As
my dad likes to say, "There's only one God, and you're not Him."
Every other human soul falls short. Understanding our limitations
gives us perspective on our significance here on earth and on our
dependency on a greater Source who can do more than our ambitions by themselves. Good intentions are commendable unless
they lead to false or impossible expectations. Overcommitting is a
lie that we tell ourselves, resulting in the disappointment of others.
The more we commit to the impossible, the more we will lose
influence and credibility. We must choose our opportunities carefully and increase our understanding of our limitations in order for
true change to occur in our lives.

It is time we all faced this truth: I can't do it all. You can't do it
all. Not every opportunity is a good opportunity. Not every social
gathering I'm invited to will be right (or possible) for me to attend.

Not every person I meet will become a good friend. No one can do it all. So don't try.

My brother-in-law Mike Morin taught me numerous principles in life and in business over the years. I interned with him for two years in college while he was a partner at an integrated marketing firm called The Image Group in Holland, Michigan. Those summers were foundational to my creative process today. Mike's mind is unmatched when it comes to innovation and problem solving.

I will never forget the sign posted in his office. The sign featured three words: "CHEAP, FAST, GREAT."

It had one instruction below the three words: "Pick two."

Mike taught me that we can never have all three in business and life. If you choose fast and great, your project, whatever it is, will never be cheap. If you choose cheap and fast, it can't be guaranteed to be great. If you choose cheap and great, it will rarely be completed as fast as you want. Sadly, we always want all three, and we won't take no for an answer.

Many of our work environments are committed to quality pricing, rapid results, and high performance. But we cannot physically do it all. We either overpromise or underdeliver, or we meet all three demands and ruin our families and relationships in the process. Our attempts to be all things to all people often result in personal exhaustion, overcommitment, and failure.

The word *fast* has become a given in American society. Historians point to westward expansion in the 1800s as the birthplace for the American love of speed. Everyone wanted to be the first one to the new land, and their chase to be first wreaked as much havoc then as it does now. Estimates say that as many as one-third of the high-pressure steam-engine boats built to navigate the Mississippi as quickly as possible were lost to accidents—most from explosions resulting from overheated engines running at full throttle for too long. The American motto: "Go ahead anyhow."[3]

Fast-forward two hundred years, and we haven't changed. We still go full steam ahead, recklessly ignoring the many signs warning of impending disaster. We've become a drive-thru culture, and we all know that a drive-thru rarely creates great, healthy food. We learned by watching the famous documentary *Super Size Me*.[4] But how often do we either consciously or unconsciously say, "Go ahead anyhow"? We need to realize our mental, physical, and emotional limitations so that we can realistically determine how much time is enough. The greater our understanding of our personal limitations, the closer we find ourselves to our calling. Pick two.

QUIT ON THURSDAY

Andre and I left on a weekend getaway to experience the city of Austin, Texas, to celebrate my thirty-first birthday and to cheer the fact that we made it through our first year of raising a child.

When we sat down for my birthday dinner the conversation began. I was not fulfilling my role as a husband and father, and even as she told me, I knew it. As I tried to manage all of my responsibilities in life I had lost track of that which was most important to me. That dinner conversation resulted in one of the biggest arguments of our marriage. When it came down to it, we both felt exhausted. I was not prioritizing her. We sought to meet the needs of others before prioritizing one another and the needs of our growing family. I selfishly pursued everything else around me, which hindered my relationship with the person I love most. I remember lying in bed that night with tears running down my face, realizing that I was wrong. I wanted to please so many people, and I simply couldn't do it. I had failed to say no to others and yes to her. On the greatest commitment of my life, I had underdelivered. We all have moments in our lives when time stands still and we're forced to make a decision about how to move forward. This was one of those moments for me. It was time to change.

Bob Goff is a mentor of mine who has such a fresh outlook on life. I shared my struggle with him. He looked at me without flinching and said, "Then quit. It's Thursday—quit."

I was more than a little surprised to hear him say that. I'm not a quitter. I couldn't quite process what he was saying.

Incredulous, I asked, "What do you mean, Bob?"

He shared that with the first couple of jobs he had, he quit, and both times he quit, it was on a Thursday. Once he saw the pattern, he created a new weekly ritual. Now, every Thursday morning he wakes up and asks himself, "What is currently in my life that is taking away from what I am made to do? There are many things that we can do, but only few that we are made to do." If he thinks of something, he quits. How can we keep moving forward if we're still doing things that take away from what we are designed to do and be? It is a simple decision. He found a way to take the emotion out of the situation by determining that Thursdays are good days to quit. Then he put the question to me: "It is Thursday, Jeff—what do you need to quit?"

The more Andre and I thought about this idea, the more it resonated with what we needed. We realized that many of the activities in our lives had a big start-up strategy and no exit strategy. We hadn't built in time to reevaluate any number of the commitments in our lives. We kept adding activities and responsibilities without considering what was most important.

You may be in a similar position. What is in your life today that needs an exit strategy? The truth is that others will not provide you an exit strategy. Only you can determine the ending points for your activities. Learn to say no. Quit … it's Thursday.

Andre and I felt that not only did we need to quit one thing—we needed to quit almost everything. We needed time and space to work through our direction and priorities. Our commitments had overtaken our ability to evaluate our priorities. We both knew that this type of change wouldn't happen immediately, so we agreed to a few things that we could implement quickly to soften the situation. We created a progression for the year ahead to take a retreat from everything. Over the course of ten months, we prepared to "stop everything" and save up money to make the time and space we needed. I actually remember looking at Andre month after month in preparation and saying, "How are we going to do this? How are the finances going to work out?" We would console each another, saying, "We have no idea how it's going to work, but we can't afford not to do it." Bob even said to us, "Now, I know you are worried about the finances. What is the worse thing that can happen? You can't eat? If you can't eat, call me. I will make sure you get food." He made us laugh. We moved forward. We were all in. We geared up for a three-month sabbatical to reevaluate our lives.

Initially, we quit the easy things and approached the harder things over time as we gained confidence. We quit being ushers on Sundays at our church. We quit leading a small group. We quit consulting with four different businesses. I vowed to quit being involved in any drama (seriously, it's amazing how much time and energy drama can take up in our lives). We quit our Thursday-morning Bible study. And so on. Andre went to her boss and explained our plan and how we'd decided to take a break from work. She was willing to quit, but her boss was extremely gracious and told her to take the time and she would have a job when she returned. So we quit everything. We stopped doing everything and chose to do nothing. We needed a new perspective on what to prioritize with our time.

We moved to Nicaragua for nine weeks, where we didn't know anyone. We didn't have an agenda. We needed to stop. A team of people supported us with prayer and guidance during that time. Through their wisdom, we processed the following questions:

Our family matters—how do we prioritize this in our lives first?

What are our personal callings and dreams? How do we make those important?

What brings us life, and how do we proactively plan that into our schedules?

After quitting everything, what do we miss? Let's do those things.

After quitting everything, what do we not miss? Let's not do those things.

What is important to us but sucks away our energy? How can we create boundaries for healthy lives?

Who makes us desire things that we don't need? Who helps us desire the things that really matter? How do we balance these relationships?

After processing these questions together, we created some boundaries for moving forward. We called these boundaries "rhythms." Our rhythms are custom-made for our lives, so the way we use our time must be unique to us. We all need a pace in our lives that matches our priorities, needs, and dreams and helps us pursue life in a healthy manner.

BACK TO WORK

We returned back to our home, our dog, our friends, and our jobs, and we tried out these rhythms in real life. It was one thing to create the rhythms that felt right when we were away … but another thing altogether to determine what was realistic in our regular everyday lives.

Regular conversations kept an open dialogue between us the first month as we reintegrated into our community. It was messy, but we committed to live differently. My superhero (overinflated view of myself) tendencies presented a conflict almost immediately. Caught up in the flow of a conversation, I remember quickly saying yes to speaking to two groups on two consecutive nights of the week. Then I told Andre what I had promised. She said no. And she was right. Sometimes, these sticky situations offered the catalyst for aha moments.

As I pondered my dilemma, because I hate having to call someone back to change my answer, I realized that every opportunity not right for me brings an opportunity for someone else. When I claim more than what I can handle, I limit the opportunities for another person in my community. In essence, when we choose to do what we ought to do, forsaking all else, we create opportunities and access for others.

So when I declined the speaking opportunity, I asked if I could recommend a friend of mine who would be incredible for their gathering. This created access in a new opportunity for him, allowing him to continue doing everything he is meant to do. My no turned into someone else's yes.

THE GIFT OF OPPORTUNITY

Have you ever stopped to think about how you have arrived where you are today? I guarantee you that someone gave you an opportunity. Someone believed in your abilities and gave you a platform to live out what it is that makes you breathe today. Don't we all want to be part of a community that has the best interest of others at its heart?

The greatest love you can give friends is to help them find and achieve their calling. Let me say that again. The greatest responsibility I have as a friend is to help others discover what only they are made to do. We all find ourselves wanting more when we do not have a confirmation of our calling. We mask the unrest in our souls by wearing clothes and accessories that make us feel good. Deep inside, however, we still long to understand our purpose and passion in life. I feel it, you feel it, and our friends feel it too. Honestly, I want others to pull out of me every reason I've been designed to walk this earth. In order for this to happen, I have to give others opportunities to succeed as well.

I want to be involved in a community that does everything possible to help one another find the unique value that only they can contribute to the world. I want to be a part of a community that works together to create platforms for that talent. I want to do less so my friends can do what only they can do.

When you think about your aspirations for your closest friends, do you really want them to succeed? Are you willing to celebrate their victories the way you'd celebrate your own? Wouldn't you love to join a community of people helping each other pursue their dreams, aspirations, and purposes?

It starts with you, and it starts with me.

Let's create a community that is deeply alive. As you walk through your day, think about the people you love and those whom you ought to pursue. How can you use your influence to help them succeed? What access do you have that can further the calling of a friend? When you give your opportunities and energy to serve the calling of others, everyone wins.

The gap between who we are and who we are designed to be is often bridged by a combination of individual pursuit and a friend giving us an opportunity. I would not do what I do today if it weren't for numerous others who saw potential in me. People like Brad Lockwood. He gave me endless time and attention in high school, saw my abilities before I did, and helped me along my journey (he always took my phone calls when I needed him). Dr. Gayle Beebe met me late in the evening after his entire family went to sleep to share what it means to lead with character and love for people. Marcia Piper let me experiment with business ideas before I knew how to sustain a business. Mike Morin brought me along to every meeting he had and let me experience what it meant to do business, even when I said the wrong thing. Robin Small gave me my first internship and taught me what it means to understand people as a starting place for marketing ideas. Her husband, Kevin Small, placed me in a position of influence before I was ready to lead. Gabe Lyons took me under his wing and taught me what it means to connect with people and put their projects at the top of my agenda. The list of people who believed enough in my abilities to put their influence on the line and raise my potential is long.

TIME FOR THE LEAST OF THESE

One of the shared priorities Andre and I keep is to make time and space in our lives for those in need. "Mother Teresa lived by a belief that there is a physical, emotional, and spiritual need in every community," wrote Brandon Hatmaker. "Need is everywhere, yet we too often fail to see it. If we don't see it, we won't be bothered by it.

If we're not bothered by it, we won't engage it. By our neglect, we become the oppressor."[5]

Our desires consume our time. But when we prioritize our time to help people in great need, our desires change drastically. When we choose to take time to be friends with people who see the world from a different perspective, we begin to see the world from a different perspective. I think as a society we are good at volunteering. As the next generation becomes more and more passionate about service, we dig into the lives of people and serve needs in our communities. But the next level of friendship requires us to break the barrier of a separated lifestyle and begin to integrate their lives into ours.

Since moving to Atlanta, we've prioritized an annual trip to visit the Martin Luther King Jr. National Historic Site.[6] One thing that continually intrigues me is where King lived and how his city fueled the broader vision he communicated. Every day as he walked out of his home he interacted with the needs of real people in the streets of Atlanta, while also rubbing shoulders with the most influential. His downtown neighborhood encompassed a peculiar mix of the working poor, the upwardly mobile middle class, and the wealthier city influencers. I have to believe the streets affected him as he walked through downtown, soaking in the hopelessness of the unseen and the swagger of the powerful.

King became a voice for the people who were not normally heard, and he used his influence to spotlight the greatest needs of his time. He was a voice for those pushed to the back of the bus, for those who couldn't speak out, for those in society oppressed just because of the color of their skin. My yearly trip reminds me that I must see the oppressed of today and be a voice for them. As I gain access, I never want to forget my responsibility to forge pathways of access for others.

We have so many opportunities to bring someone along on our journey. It could be as simple as inviting a teenager with us to a local sports game. Perhaps we could pay for a young leader to go to a leadership conference with us. We could invite a friend to a business meeting to listen in on the conversation. We could hire an intern to share our knowledge. We could bring along new friends to meet old friends at a party.

What if our understanding of access changed? Access is a gift granted to us for the sake of others. What if every time we were granted an opportunity to do something special we first thought about who we could take along with us to experience this special event? In every circle in which we gain access, may we invite another person along with us.

LEBRON JAMES, NICK CANNON, AND DARRIUS SNOW

Vince Hungate leads an organization called Essential2Life,[7] for which I was a board member for three years. They started a program called Fifteen. Fifteen is three-year program for high school students that focuses on developing the students as leaders who will positively influence their communities. Fifteen chose these students because they had natural influence in their classes already and just needed some additional opportunities for personal growth and mentorship. I remember asking Vince what he saw as the students' greatest need. Without skipping a beat, Vince shared how these students have unending potential, yet they lack access to networks of influence. Most of their families never had opportunities outside of their current situations. In today's economy, their greatest need is to be introduced to people who can offer them opportunity.

Darrius Snow was one of those teenagers.

Darrius was born in the projects of Atlanta, is one of five kids (each with a different father), and was abandoned by his drug-addicted mother when he was two years old.

"Growing up in my neighborhood was challenging, and I didn't have much of a childhood," he said. "I struggled repeatedly and at times I even fell, but I picked myself up and kept going, knowing there's always salvation on the other side of my obstacle."[8]

Darrius is the first of his family to graduate high school, and he'll finish his degree at Voorhees College soon, with plans to study next at Harvard. His potential is endless; he just needed a couple of opportunities. He started right where he was by establishing Bankhead Teens Encouraging Action by Motivating others. The BTEAM's mission is "to transform their neighborhood from a drug and crime-infested area, to a positive environment where young people can grow towards a brighter future."[9] He made his dream happen when he received an unexpected opportunity. Essential2Life applied on his behalf for the TeenNick HALO awards, which spotlight people making a difference in their communities. After a series of reviews, Darrius was selected as a finalist. He boarded a plane for the first time and headed to Ohio to share his story with some kids much like him. During the trip he met the host, Nick Cannon.

What Darrius didn't realize was that this single weekend would dramatically change his story forever. After talking to the Nickelodeon cameras about BTEAM, Cannon told Snow that he was one of four people chosen for the network's first TeenNick HALO Award. The award came with a ten thousand dollar grant for Snow's projects, a ten thousand dollar scholarship, and a weekend with NBA star LeBron James.[10] That weekend was a dream for an eighteen-year-old rising star.

Darrius now regularly talks to one of the most influential basketball players in the world. Darrius already created a new trajectory for his family, but he got help through increased access and opportunity, which was exactly what he needed. Today, he has expanded his organization to a mentoring program with hundreds of mentoring relationships. He turned his access into access for other people.

MORE OR LESS ACCESS

When we look at where we are in life, we usually focus on the place we want to be and what it takes to get to that place. Right? We dream of what it will feel like to *arrive*. That's a good thing. We should never stop dreaming and reaching. However, our greatest responsibility in community is to do everything we can to help others find who God designed them to be. Are you using your unique access to further your own personal gain, or do you freely give of that access to others?

Give an opportunity of access to someone who needs a special boost in his or her journey. Dale Carnegie said, "You can make more friends in two months by becoming genuinely interested in other people than you can in two years by trying to get other people interested in you."[11] Do you have access? Take someone with you.

ENOUGH TALK

In the week ahead, look at your calendar and determine which events or activities on your schedule are most exciting to you. For each event, find a person to take with you who you think could benefit from the opportunity. Give someone else access to a new opportunity. This experiment is simple—just share your experience with others.

[10]

BLACK & RED

We don't think ourselves into a new way of living;
we live ourselves into a new way of thinking.

—*Richard Rohr*

I've been processing the question "What is enough?" for several years, and the way I see the world is changing. I am writing this in the wake of Black Friday. Black Friday, of course, is the shopping day that follows Thanksgiving every year in America. It is also a day that brings back many memories for me.

I was a newspaper carrier in Lansing, Michigan, for six years, delivering the *Lansing State Journal* for seven days a week to about a hundred doors and porches before seven o'clock in the morning. I started when I was just twelve years old—a young kid wanting to make some money to buy video games. I made fifty dollars per week—not bad money for a twelve-year-old.

Looking back, it was a special time for me because from the first day on the job, my dad woke up and did the paper route with me. He willingly chose to spend about two thousand hours of his life alongside me, investing in my entrepreneurial spirit. We woke up and folded all the papers (bagging them on rainy days), then lined them up in large over-the-shoulder bags with florescent orange shoulder straps, and started walking through the neighborhood. We each carried two bags at a time, one on each shoulder, and balanced with every step.

The most dreaded day of the entire year was Thanksgiving Day. While most of teenage America slept in and dreamed of turkey, apple pies, and football, we woke up even earlier than usual to roll and deliver the thickest and heaviest paper of the year. Back before the current proliferation of social media, every Black Friday deal was revealed in the newspaper on Thanksgiving Day. Translation: every carrier's Black Friday came a day early.

After we finished our deliveries, the fun part of that day for me was kicking my feet up in our old orange La-Z-Boy and starting the annual treasure hunt for deals.

Reading through that newspaper felt like living in my own Choose Your Own Adventure book. Determine the treasure you want to find and decide what you're willing to do to get it. How early will you wake up to win? Will you sleep overnight, in line, with your close friends outside the store? Who can you convince to accompany you? I opened those papers and started dreaming an epic story of the chase. My imagination ran wild with the pursuit, wondering what I would do with the new gadget in the following days. It started in junior high (when I would have to convince my family to take me), progressed into high school (when I would bribe brother-in-laws by buying them breakfast after shopping), and stayed with me into college when I convinced Andre how amazing the deals were and how we could get all our Christmas shopping done in one day. Of course, the day's shopping always included one treasure for me along the way.

Black Friday. Have you ever wondered where this term originated? I discovered two explanations for why they call it Black Friday. The *American Philatelist* dates it back to 1966 in Philadelphia: "'Black Friday' is the name which the Philadelphia Police Department has given to the Friday following Thanksgiving Day. It is not a term of endearment to them. 'Black Friday' officially opens the Christmas shopping season in center city, and it usually brings massive traffic jams and over-crowded sidewalks as the downtown stores are mobbed from opening to closing."[1] On November 26, 1982, the general population started using the term and it was elevated to a national holiday of sorts when Dan Cordtz referred to it on *World News Tonight*: "Some merchants label the day after Thanksgiving 'Black Friday' because business today can mean the difference between red ink and black on the ledgers."[2] This is the second explanation for the term *Black Friday*. When accountants use the phrase *in the black*, it means that a company is making a profit. The opposite phrase is *in the red*, which means the company is losing money. Retailers hope that regardless of how the rest of the year has gone, in that final month of the year, largely because of Black Friday, a company will end profitable. Prior to Black Friday, retailers often have an excess of inventory. Store managers and corporate owners hope to use Black Friday deals to entice consumers to purchase their products so they will finish the year in the black. Of course, retailers often convince us to use money we don't have to make up for their losses, resulting in red for us and black for them.

Red and black.

These colors evoke such clear visual and emotional responses. Pablo Picasso once said that "colors, like features, follow the changes of emotions." Have you ever heard of the psychology of colors? Colors have meaning and trigger emotional responses. Just think about the three colors of a stoplight: red (stop), green (go), yellow (slow down or step on the gas). Now think about the meanings of black and red.

Black. We know that in the financial or business realm, black means profitable. Black is the color of authority, stability, and strength. Some associate the color black with intelligence and success (think black robe, black belt, black-rimmed glasses). If you want to look skinnier, you wear black. It's also a somber color equated with grief or loss, such as when we wear black to funerals. Black is also a color you wear to a fancy, upscale "black tie" event.

Red. In the financial or business world red refers to a loss, anything less than enough. If you want others to notice you, use the color red—our eyes are drawn to look at red first. Red is an energetic color. Wearing red clothes will make you appear a bit heavier and certainly more noticeable. Tiger Woods is famous for wearing red on Sundays. When a man wears a red tie, they refer to it as a power tie, a tie that means the man is looking to make something happen. When we think of blood, we immediately think of a deep red. But, we also use red for love and giving (think red roses, Valentine's hearts, Christmas, etc.).[3]

Red and black both signify life and death, good and evil, and even winning and losing. Both colors evoke deep emotion, meaning, and interpretation. For our purposes in this book, black and red are the colors I will choose to define enough.

IN THE RED

If we are "in the red" as a business, we're fighting for survival and in need of something more to keep going. This applies to other areas of life as well. And this great need can inspire resilience, renewed life, and ambition to overcome massive, seemingly impossible obstacles. When we need more and can't do it on our own, a deep faith emerges as we call out to greater powers for help. In these times, we quickly grasp the value of what matters most, and we value happiness that much more. These red moments of desperation, in business or otherwise, can reveal the most beautiful things in life. When we are in the red, hope shines bright. This is when we long for others to stand with us, and we offer ourselves transparently, desperate for something more. It is in these moments when songwriters write the greatest music, filmmakers shoot the most honest films, painters create masterful canvases, and writers create stories of hope. Ironically, out of our most desperate need to survive we can experience life. These red moments in our lives bring opportunity and ambition to find another way forward.

Everyone has a different reason why they might choose to pursue (or not pursue) the question of enough that we're tackling in this book. My personal faith is my greatest motivation for answering this question in my own life. Regardless of your faith background, I think we can all respect the life and teaching of Jesus. Through His life, Jesus consistently focused His attention on people whose lives were in the red, so to speak. He often talked about the poor and always brought hope to people in despair. In Luke 6:20–21, Jesus taught this message: "Blessed are you who are poor, for yours is the kingdom of God. Blessed are you who hunger now, for you will be satisfied. Blessed are you who weep now, for you will laugh." Jesus spoke words of hope to those living in need, living in the red. He assured them that they were blessed and that someday their desires would be fulfilled. Jesus saw the power of being in the red: *hope.*

On a very practical level, Jesus also taught that everyone has something to give: rich or poor, far in the black or deep in the red. In Mark 12:41–44, He celebrated the willingness of a poor widow to give not out of her abundance, but out of her poverty:

> Jesus sat down opposite the place where the offerings were put and watched the crowd putting their money into the temple treasury. Many rich people threw in large amounts. But a poor widow came and put in two very small copper coins, worth only a fraction of a penny.

> Calling his disciples to him, Jesus said, "I tell you the truth, this poor widow has put more into the treasury than all the others. They all gave out of their wealth; but she, out of her poverty, put in everything—all she had to live on."

While most of us will never give to others out of such dire poverty, we rarely consider ourselves rich. Is it possible that Jesus was trying to help us rethink our definitions of enough in that moment? It's time we begin to see our excess with new perspective.

Author and strategist Tim Sanders would say that most of us are rich, living in the black. His grandmother taught him this principle at an early age in life: "By being able and willing to give, we are rich. There's bank-account rich, and there's rich in spirit. The second kind is achieved when you make a difference. It's the forever kind of rich that no one can take away from you.... Rich means the cup's got enough in it to quench my thirst. More than enough."[4]

We each have the opportunity to contribute whatever we are willing to share—gifts big or small. Sometimes the smallest of gifts makes the largest difference. Regardless of the size, the issue is our willingness to give. Even when we live in the red, we have the opportunity to contribute, as demonstrated by the widow in Mark 12. Even out of our poverty we have the opportunity to give to others.

Have you ever noticed that in some Bibles, Jesus's words are printed in red? I always wondered who started the trend.

A quick Internet search brought up a fascinating story about a newspaper publisher by the name of Louis Klopsch. He often printed the sermons written by his mentor, Dr. Talmage, for wider publication:

> On June 19, 1899, while composing an editorial, his eye fell upon Luke 22:20: "This cup is the new testament in my blood, which I shed for you." Seizing upon the symbolism of blood, Klopsch asked Dr. Talmage if Christ's words could not be printed in red. His mentor replied: "It could do no harm and it most certainly could do much good." ...
>
> An initial edition of 60,000 "Red Letter Testaments" was soon sold out. Accolades streamed in, from the King of Sweden (a telegram) to President Theodore Roosevelt (a dinner invitation which Louis Klopsch accepted).
>
> Klopsch also pioneered American overseas charities in a massive fashion, raising more than three million dollars through his newspaper. He aided famine victims in many places such as Sweden and Japan.[5]

As we look at things like red-letter innovation and addressing the needs of hunger in the world, you can see that I'm not advocating anything new. Jesus's words back then prompted His followers to define enough and use their excess to make a difference. His words do the same for me and many others today.

As we seek to answer the question "What is enough?" we must consider red the color of desperation, hope, and opportunity to serve the needs of others.

IN THE BLACK

Recently while driving home, I talked on the phone with my friend Brian. We talked about some last-second plans for our upcoming business trip. He and three friends planned to pick me up on the way to a creative retreat for Catalyst (the next-generation leadership conference). It was 9:15 a.m. on a weekday. I got out of my car and locked it behind me, messenger bag on my left shoulder. My left hand held a cup of black coffee brewed at a coffee shop a mile down the road. It was still hot. The conversation continued, my phone pinned between my right shoulder and my right ear. My house keys sat in my right hand.

You can imagine the circus-level balancing act I performed as I tried to get the keys in the door without dropping everything at the same time. I opened the door and had started walking back to my bedroom when I suddenly noticed that all the drawers in the kitchen had been pulled out. The contents of the drawers littered the floor and the counters. I looked up and saw my dog, Maximus, standing on our back porch, looking through a huge hole in the glass of our back doors. Shattered glass was everywhere. I don't remember what Brian and I were talking about at that moment, but I know what I said to him next.

"Hey, Brian … can you stay on the phone with me?—our house got broken into," I stammered. "I don't think I can go on the trip. I got robbed."

Looking back at the situation, I felt extremely calm only because I was on the phone with Brian. I am thankful he was on the other end and, in a way, was with me. I started to survey the house. The back door was busted. Three computers—*stolen*. The envelope system we used to organize cash—*gone*. My change jar—*empty*. Our bedroom and closets—*a mess*. Our roommate's bike—*missing*. Our iPods—*nowhere*. On top of that, Andre had left her purse in the house that day. It was obviously taken—all her identification, passport, and credit cards … *vanished*. The list went on and on. In total, over ten thousand dollars worth of assets, gone at nine o'clock in the morning.

My next memory was of sitting on our front porch with the front door open, waiting for the police to show up. Andre was on her way home to check out the damages. I was on hold, waiting to talk to one of my credit-card companies to cancel our cards. While I waited, I looked in every direction, mad at every neighbor I could see as I tried to figure out why not a single person had stopped the robbery. My neighbor across the street was home but hadn't seen a thing. My neighbor next door didn't even know it happened.

Caught in this twilight zone and unsure what to do next, I started thinking about what I lost and what I still had that day. I didn't lose my family. I didn't lose my job. I didn't lose my dignity or even my character. I lost money and a few conveniences. Most of the things I lost I could easily replace. It may take a little time, but it wasn't the end of the world. The only true losses were the pictures on our computer that we had not backed up. Everything else we easily replaced.

I'll never forget that day.

I often sit on my front porch and think about that morning and the emotions of the day. It was both a sad day and a day of liberation. It was the day that our house was robbed, but it was also the day I realized that, for the most part, I live in the black. I like my stuff, but the world won't end if I don't have all of my stuff forever. Most of my stuff can also be easily replaced. That day helped me mourn in a way, when I realized how attached I was to the things that I own. Afterward, I came to the conclusion that my stuff is not my own. I have dominion over many things and have a responsibility to care for them. But those things may not be mine forever. There are times when others need what I own more than I do and times when they will be taken away. My stuff is not me.

Later that morning, I talked with Leroy Barber. Leroy is the president of Mission Year and CEO of FCS Urban Ministries, and he's mentored me on how to live in the city and love my neighbors. I told him the story of what happened. He didn't ask if I was okay. He didn't ask what was taken. He didn't ask about my emotions. He asked me one question: "Are you going to continue living in your house?"

I answered quickly, "Yes!" There was never a doubt in my mind.

He responded, "Welcome to the neighborhood."

Leroy went on to tell me about numerous people he's known who have moved into developing neighborhoods, and inevitably something bad happened. They often respond by deserting the neighborhood altogether and going back to what is comfortable and safe. Leroy helped me process the reality that when we engage in the messiness and tension of a suffering community, we experience the positive and negative ways that people respond to that suffering. As a result, we live in the tension between desperation and excess; while we live in the black, others fight for survival in the red. This becomes a real aspect of community: struggling through loving our neighbors when our neighbors do not enjoy the same blessings we do.

As advocates for living a life wrestling with "what is enough?" we claim the color black. We see in the color black opportunity, struggle, and the future, which consists of giving up claim to our unnecessary excess and living in freedom. Choosing enough is not only living the good life: it is a life of doing the most good.[6]

A DIFFERENT SALE

One day, I sat down for coffee with a friend coming through Atlanta. His name is Chris Marlow, and he lives in Austin, Texas, where he helps keep Austin weird in his own unique way. Chris is the type of person many of us wish we were. He is a quiet leader who follows what he believes with his heart and with his steps. If he learns about a need in the world, he begins to live his life in a way that finds a solution.

Chris started an organization called HelpOneNow.[7] HelpOneNow is a global tribe dedicated to ending extreme poverty by helping to *rescue* orphans, *restore* their hope, and *renew* their communities. Chris shared with me that he wanted to find a funding model for orphan care different from the wildly successful child sponsorship model. He didn't want to replicate what's already been done but instead wanted to find new streams of funding to help even more children who are desperate to meet their basic needs. Even though child sponsorship currently works well, he believes there is a need to find new solutions to meet this global need.

So we started brainstorming.

I asked him if his community had innovated any creative solutions to the fund-raising strategy. He told me about a church that had sent him a check for eight hundred dollars out of the blue. Eight hundred dollars would support an orphan in their program for nearly two years. Chris found out that this church had simply put together a garage sale, and all the proceeds went toward orphans—a single church raised over eight hundred dollars on one Saturday morning. Two other churches had done similar things and sent Chris checks for over a thousand dollars each. Meanwhile, Chris racked his brain for a creative way to raise funds for orphans. I sat back and just kind of laughed because he didn't need any new ideas from me or anyone else. His community could adopt a new fund-raising strategy for HelpOneNow using this creative but simple idea. That day marked the start of Garage Sale for Orphans.[8]

I can't think of a better example of the ideas we're talking about in this book: out of our excess we can address issues of need and suffering. Chris and his community adopted a "simple way for everyone to get involved and help orphans and communities who are struggling due to extreme poverty."[9] We can all host a garage sale. What a great way to bring together a community, clean out our excess junk, and contribute to the betterment of others. It's a perfect way to teach the principles of "what is enough?" to kids, schools, churches, small groups, youth groups, businesses, families, and individuals. The Garage Sale for Orphans initiative asks all of us to look into our closets, find the stuff that we do not need, sell it, and contribute it to a great cause. As a community, people in Austin now pull together their excess and sell it to help rescue abandoned children. This innovative strategy has turned into over a hundred thousand dollars given to children, and Chris plans to raise over one million dollars in the next three years. Our excess has the opportunity to be turned into survival and freedom.

To me it's like the Black Friday strategy that retailers use every year: we sell off our own excess, resulting in extra cash for those in need. That's a sale worth getting up early in the morning to celebrate. When was the last time you had a garage sale?

POSITIVE & NEGATIVE

At the risk of oversimplifying, let's define some terms. More than enough is excess. Less than enough is suffering. Most of us either have a positive or a negative balance. *More or less*. I believe the most difficult and yet important question for our generation is to determine what is enough in each and every aspect of our lives. We should keep a figurative balance sheet for everything that consumes our money, time, energy, concentration, and other things. Then you can ask yourself, what is my balance today? Are you in the red, or are you in the black?

We will either be consumed by culture or will choose to define enough by our personal conscience. The good life is not found in luxury; rather it is found in a life that enhances the life of another human. We will become known by the choices we make because people will see the lifestyle that we live and how we give to others. If we have more than enough, we have the opportunity to bless others. This is the start to living a life of generosity. You see, generosity is not about giving money. Generosity is a lifestyle that seeks to understand the needs of others and strives to bring an end to that suffering. True generosity is a choice: when those of us living in the black choose to live with less so others can have more. If we choose generosity, we place the interests and needs of others above our own personal gain. To freely give something that you care about to another human is a great act of humility. The founder of TOMS Shoes, Blake Mycoskie, said, "Whoever you are and whatever you do, giving is important. Start now. Start by helping other people—anyone you can…. Commit to seeing the world through the lens of how you can initiate meaningful change."[10]

More and less. Black and red. Excess and suffering. It is in the tension, the process, the discovering, the uncovering, the traveling, and the questioning that we find who we are and discover what we are meant to become.

ENOUGH TALK

Preparing a garage sale and implementing it may take an extended period of time. But there is something you can do quickly and efficiently that can provide you a similar experience. Look around your home and choose one item that you currently own that is valued at more than fifty dollars. It may be a chair, a video-game system you don't use anymore, a bread-making machine, or maybe even an old baseball card. Figure out the value of the item and post it for sale online through the numerous sale sites that exist today. Use social media to get the word out to your friends about the sale and the cause you want to support with the proceeds.

Then give whatever you receive from that sale to a local need in your community. This is a simple way to understand the excess we have and the needs we can solve today quickly and efficiently while limiting the stuff in our cupboards.

[11]

ENOUGH GIFT CARDS

Success is the point where your most authentic
talents, passion, values, and experiences intersect
with the chance to contribute to some greater good.

—*Bill Strickland*, Make the Impossible Possible

Andre and I married the summer after we graduated from Spring
Arbor University and were blessed by the people that supported
us on that special day on August 17, 2002. After opening all of
our gifts and greeting cards, we had a stack of gift cards sitting on
the table. In total we had about forty gift cards for either Target
or Bed Bath & Beyond, two fine establishments that we visited
frequently. We realized after stocking up that there was literally
nothing left that we wanted to buy. And we still had a stack of
cards sitting on top of our bedroom dresser. It was kind of crazy.
We had prepurchased money sitting on cards and nothing to do
with it. We looked at each other and declared that we had more
than enough. We were blessed far beyond our needs. Our friends

and family had blessed us with unending gifts, and they gave us so much that we had an excess of gift cards.

I wondered how many of my friends had gift cards like this just sitting around. I came up with a theory. Every person I know has a gift card that just sits on their dresser, in their wallet, or in their purse. They simply don't have any specific thing they want to buy. Or maybe they use a gift card at a store but don't know what to do with the last $1.32 left on the card. Perhaps it's a restaurant gift card, and that restaurant doesn't have a location near where they live, so they can't use it. Maybe they know that if they spend that gift card, they will actually spend more than is on the card, forcing them over a budget.

This theory bounced around in my head for many years. Andre and I would talk about what we could do if we gathered that money. Andre is a deeply compassionate person and realized her desire to help others in need at an early stage in her life. In our marriage counseling, she told me about her desire to create a savings account specifically for others, which she called the giving fund. She dreamed of hearing about a friend who got a flat tire and had no money to pay for the replacement. We would withdraw a hundred dollars cash from our special account, stick it in an envelope, and slip it under their door anonymously. What mattered to Andre was meeting our friend's specific need so he or she could move on with a smile. Her hope was that this person would feel so blessed, he or she would feel compelled to pass that generosity onto another person who needed it.

Like many of our friends, we had school debt, and at the time Andre was preparing to attend Emory University to earn her master's degree. The idea of the giving fund coming to life anytime soon was not realistic. But what if we could do a similar thing with gift cards? What if our theory was right? What if people would give us their leftover or unused gift cards and we could help people in need with the proceeds? It seemed unrealistic to us both until we attended some friends' wedding.

Have you ever attended a wedding reception and sat down at a table full of strangers? It's always a bit awkward, but usually by the end of the night you have some pretty interesting conversations because you have one thing in common: *the friends getting married*. On this particular day, the conversation at the table wasn't exactly flowing. I asked every question that I could, and we all had nothing in common. So I decided to test out my theory on some complete strangers.

"So I have this theory …" I began.

Before I knew it, three of the women pulled out their purses, and a couple of guys started sifting through their wallets.

"I have ten dollars on this card," one guy said.

"I have six seventy-eight left on this one," another said.

"I have thirty-seven cents."

We totaled the amount of all the cards, and it was over fifty dollars. So the bigger question was this: would they be willing to give a complete stranger these gift cards? I reassured them that if they chose to trust us, we promised we would give them to someone in need. We would only give them to a person who could use the money on the cards to get out of a difficult situation. Without flinching, each of them tossed us the gift cards. We couldn't believe it. In that moment, we realized that people want to use what they have to help the needs of others. We had just found a simple way to give to others, and collectively we could do something extraordinary.

GiftCardGiver.com was born.

On our way home from the wedding we called our friends Jason and Heather Locy to tell them the news about our experiment. While we were on the phone Jason started looking up URLs for the website. Jason owns a phenomenal creative agency and design team called Fivestone.[1] They offered to freely help us make a website to start to share the story and the idea with others. Within a month we had our story online. We emailed friends to get feedback, and over and over again we heard, "That's a good idea …why didn't I think of that?" When you have a good idea, people will let you know. I believe when you have a good idea it matters to people, because it addresses a social need. People will not forget a good idea; rather, they will share it.

When we researched the gift-card industry, we found some staggering statistics. Did you know that last year an estimated one hundred billion dollars was spent on gift cards in America?[2] Birthdays are the number-one occasion for gift cards. Two-thirds of all Americans have purchased at least one gift card. And it makes sense for retailers to use them, because research tells us that most consumers who receive gift cards spend *more* than the card's original value.[3] So this industry pays off in the end. On the other end of the spectrum, 10 to 20 percent of all gift cards purchased will never be redeemed.[4] That means that between ten and twenty billion dollars goes unused every year and is sitting on unused gift cards. Estimates say that at this moment there's more than forty-one billion dollars in unused gift cards floating around the country.[5] This dollar amount is truly staggering. Just imagine what good could be done with those resources.

Word began to travel quickly.

In a down economy, we found a revolutionary new way to raise funds for people in need. I read an article in the *Atlanta Journal-Constitution* about how nonprofits struggled with fund-raising in difficult economic times. I quickly sent an email to the author of the article, declaring that our fund-raising had never been better. We found a new way to access the excess cash sitting in the wallets and purses around the city, I wrote. It was a gutsy email, but I truly believed in the idea. He responded immediately and wanted to do a story on GiftCardGiver.com. The next week the *Atlanta Journal-Constitution* published the story, and it took off. In three weeks time, the *Atlanta Journal-Constitution,*[6] *Chicago Sun Times,* CNN,[7] Fox Business,[8] MSNBC, NPR,[9] AOL, and nineteen other national news outlets ran stories on GiftCardGiver.com. We didn't even know about half of the stories because it was Christmas and we were waiting out a snowstorm at my parents' home with no Internet access. I learned quickly that if you have a good idea that meets a social concern, people talk about it and want to share the story.

I soon became known as the gift-card guy. When we addressed social needs, we became known for the problems we tried to solve. We got interest from all over the country, and people sent gift cards from nearly every state. One card might have ninety-six dollars for Ruth's Chris Steak House, while another might have thirty-two cents for Applebee's. Every card we receive gets called on (or looked up on the Internet) to determine the actual amount left on the card. When we started, I called on all the cards, but over time we built an army of people to help call on cards. We hold calling parties, where volunteers call on our cards, checking balances for hours at a time. Several individuals give countless hours of calling time on their personal cell phones to this cause. Every great idea needs a team of people to help the idea come to life.

Friends called and asked if they could collect gift cards on our behalf. Of course, we said yes. In response to these requests, we created the Gift Card Giver House Party Kit to encourage people to invite friends to their houses for a party where everyone "gets carded" at the door. This created a collaborative opportunity for anyone to collect thousands of dollars in gift cards and give them to organizations and people in need.

Every new social venture like this one needs to learn how to scale it up, and this was our opportunity to do that. And who doesn't like a party? We wanted to do everything we could to keep it a local fund-raiser. So if you choose to host a Gift Card Giver House Party, we will seek to partner with local projects or organizations in your community. We gave the house parties simple rules, but hosts could make it as unique as they wanted. Here are the three important elements that every House Party should include:

A "bouncer" at the door to collect gift cards as the entry fee.

A wide variety of card games to entertain for the evening.

A big envelope in which to mail your stack of gift cards to Gift Card Giver.

We also connected with Chicago Bulls basketball player Kyle Korver in the summer of 2011. He wanted to help a local elementary school that was in desperate need of renovations. Kyle and his brother, Klayton Korver, placed bins all over downtown Chicago in popular restaurants and started collecting gift cards. Together they raised over six thousand dollars in gift cards over the course of just a few weeks. In turn, we used those gift cards to reward teachers for hard work, stock the classrooms full of supplies, and provide paint for walls and rugs for the floors. It's such a simple idea, but it can make such a massive difference. Churches all over the country choose to take up gift-card collections by asking their congregations to put gift cards in the offering plate as it goes around, and then they use those gift cards to help meet needs in their community. We love hearing stories about how churches met the needs of people coming through the doors of their churches by handing them a gift card for groceries or dinner.

Through all these creative techniques, we raised over a hundred thousand dollars and donated to over 230 causes, individuals, or organizations—what we call "giving stories." These stories are the *why* fueling the entire effort. Here are a few examples:

- We received a phone call from our friend Charles, who told us about women and children who were being rescued from sex trafficking. He asked if we had phone cards we could send so that these women and children could reconnect with their families. Within a matter of days we shipped *thousands* of minutes worth of phone cards to help reunite these families across the world.

- Every year we receive phone calls, letters, and emails about victims of house fires and the need to rebuild. We often contribute to those needs. Once a teacher contacted us about a little boy in her class whose house burned down. We sent his family gift cards to help buy necessities. A few weeks later we received the cutest picture of the boy holding a sign that read: "Thank you." His teacher said he'd been talking about it for days. This particular need hit close to home when friends of ours, Jill and Michelle, were the victims of a house fire. They lost everything. We were able to give them hundreds of dollars so they could buy necessities.

- After major storms or natural disasters, we gave to disaster-relief efforts in Tuscaloosa, Galveston, Atlanta, Joplin, New Orleans, and many more.

- We gave gift cards to fund a Christmas Store event for low-income families. The managers of the event used the gift cards to purchase nice items to fill the store, and then families in the neighborhood came shopping and paid much less than the value of the merchandise. This event gives them the dignity of being able to buy gifts for their families.

- A lady named Pam contacted us about her son, who has a rare genetic disease. She needed food and gas cards to drive from Alabama to Connecticut regularly for needed medical treatment. A year later Pam contacted us letting us know that two of her other children had been diagnosed with the same disease. We helped them again, providing food and gas cards for their trips to the hospital.

- We provide interview clothes for men just released from jail who are looking for work.

- We help countless nonprofit and charity organizations with gift cards to cover overhead or supply costs that other donors may not want to fund but that are essential to the work they do.

- At Christmas time, we ask people to share the names of leaders of organizations who deserve a night out. We send those leaders gift cards for movies, a nice meal, and experiences they can share with a spouse, or someone close, as a much-needed thank-you for the hard work they do.

The stories go on and on. As I step back from this project and evaluate what has happened through Gift Card Giver, I can identify several important principles we learned along the way. These principles fueled this book:

1. Out of our excess, we can address issues of need and suffering. Whether it is food, clothes, or access, most of us have some kind of excess in our lives. The question is this: will you use your excess to create more excess, or will you use it to address the needs around you?

2. We will be known by the problems we solve. Many of us guard our reputations closely. We want others to know we are honest and trustworthy. We want people to respect us. The best way we can build a reputation of worth is to look for a need and help. Everyone knows the story of the Good Samaritan. He became known for the one problem he took the time to solve. What will you be known for?

3. Influence is gained by doing something. No one ever changed the world by talking about it—they had to actually do something. If you want to make a difference, you have to start somewhere. You may fail, but at least you tried. You'll never know unless you try it, so go ahead and do something.

4. When you have a good idea, people tell you and then tell others. Your work speaks for itself. When someone sees you doing something worthwhile, they tell you: "Hey, that's a cool idea. I wish I would have thought of that." But they also tell others. You know you're doing

something right when you meet someone who says, "My friend told me all about you. Tell me more."

5. Every social innovation must learn to scale for maximum results. Don't quench the fire of a good idea by trying to control it too closely. Let the word out. Share your idea with others. Let them try it out. See what happens when you let others participate.

6. Every great idea needs a team of people to help the idea come to life. Andre and I would have had to quit our jobs in order to call on all the gift cards we've received. I couldn't design a website that would attract anyone. I only know so many people myself who can directly give me their gift cards. For an idea to make a difference beyond our spheres of influence, we need others. Take time to communicate your ideas, invite others to come with you, and enjoy the ride together.

ENOUGH TALK

Open your wallet, and pull out all your gift cards. How many do you have? How much is on each gift card? Ask your friends to do the same. Throw a house party during which everyone who comes gets "carded." Choose a charity that you would like to benefit from your Gift Card Giver House Party and designate the gift cards to go to that charity.

Send the gift cards to:

> Gift Card Giver
> PO Box 17920
> Atlanta, GA 30316

At Gift Card Giver, we will do our best to swap out the cards in order to send that charity cards they can use in the amount you collected at your party. In a really simple way, you've been able to help an organization that helps others.

To find out more about how to throw a Gift Card Giver House Party look us up online: www.giftcardgiver.com/house_party.php.

MAKING ENOUGH MORE

If we value things of the world, we will
miss the things of true value.
—Kim Biddle

We knocked on the door three times. It was a late spring Sunday afternoon in Michigan. I heard running around inside the house. Finally, someone opened the door—a boy. He held out his hand, and his face sported the brightest white smile I'd ever seen, especially in contrast with the darkest skin I'd ever seen.

"Hi, Jeff," the boy said. "Come on in. My name is Martin. We were just making some dinner."

Martin led us into the kitchen to meet everyone else. He lived with five other boys all placed in Grand Rapids, Michigan, by Bethany Christian Services. They were Sudanese refugees who came from a refugee camp in Kenya, where they'd learned the English language. My mother-in-law had introduced us to these boys, as she'd been doing routine medical checkups on each of them in the transition. Though the boys were genetically unre-lated, Bethany had placed all six of them in one house to offer a shared place of support. Bethany invited Andre and me to hang out with them one afternoon and introduce them to America. Most of the people with whom they interacted were much older, and someone thought it would be nice if they learned something of American culture from people closer to their ages. At the time, Andre and I were still in college, and we'd never met anyone quite like these boys.

As we walked into the kitchen to meet the rest of the boys, the house was full of commotion. Though only six boys lived in the house, at least twelve boys ran around as we entered: two guys sat in one room, playing a video game; one ran up and down the stairs with a soccer ball; three played dominoes at the kitchen table; one boy, wearing brand-new glasses, worked on homework with an American tutor at the kitchen table; a couple more walked in from the back door with recently collected wood in their hands.

Wait ... what are they doing with wood in their hands? I thought to myself. I hadn't seen a fireplace.

Two other boys sprawled across the floor, balling up wads of old newspaper in a pile. The wood gatherers started stacking some small wood on top of the paper. Did I mention that we were in the kitchen?

I'm sure there's some official psychological term for the slowed processing most of us experience when we walk into a new situa-tion. Unsure what to expect, we tend to mentally sit back and take it all in.

As one boy pulled out a box of matches, both Andre and I
started to wake up from our temporary mental fog. Cautiously I
said:

"Wait."

I said it a little louder: "Wait!"

Panicking: "Wait! What are you doing?"

Andre and I jumped into action just as smoke began to rise in
the middle of the kitchen.

We immediately got all the wood and newspaper out of the
kitchen and into the backyard before the house burned down.

Walking back into the kitchen, the boys looked at us, bewil-
dered. They asked innocently, "What did we do wrong? We wanted
to make you dinner." They wanted to start a fire in the middle of
the kitchen to make dinner. Andre and I looked at each other and
shared one of the biggest smiles we've ever given each other. Then
we walked over to the stove to show them how to "turn on a fire."

Their faces quickly turned to amazement. Wow.

That afternoon, they cooked us a traditional Kenyan meal
of ugali (a kind of pasty, floury substance that is sticky and used
to pick up the other food items), greens, corn, and stew. We ate
together, but I probably laughed more than I ate. These boys were
full of joy in every way, and I couldn't help but be happy in their
presence. They had a place to call home for the first time in many
years, they thoroughly enjoyed being together, and they pulled us
right into their circle. They embodied a sense of purpose in life
unlike anyone I had ever met. They all told us they came to America
to get an education and wanted to then take their profession back

to Sudan to serve the needs of the people. They were the chosen few, and they were responsible to return with blessings for their suffering friends and family.

As our friendship with those boys grew over that summer, I introduced them to American culture, for better or for worse. There were many funny stories. I taught them that toilets flush only *after* they'd filled it to the brim. They also shared about the struggle of making friends with boys who were African-American, and how none of those boys actually knew anything about Africa. When I taught multiple boys to drive, the experience was harrowing. I'm sure I shaved years off of my life after countless near misses.

And then there was the hot tub.

I asked the boys if they knew how to swim. Half knew how to swim and half did not, but none of them had ever been swimming in a pool—they'd only gone swimming in lakes, rivers, and oceans. At the time, I lived with my sister in Holland, Michigan, and she had an inground pool. One day, we asked the boys to come over for an afternoon at the pool. Sometimes you envision how a day is going to go and expect joy and happiness. That day I learned that when you are with eight teenage Sudanese refugees, the fun comes from unexpected places. We crammed eight boys looking for adventure into my sister's minivan. I imagined they would enjoy jumping on the diving board, throwing the ball around the pool, or even seeing who could surf a raft in the pool the longest. But the pool just wasn't the thing. The highlight of the afternoon was the hot tub.

Some of the tallest people on earth are Sudanese. One famous basketball player named Manute Bol stood seven-feet, six-inches tall. About half of the boys present that day came from a similar tribe. Now imagine a five-person hot tub filled with eight semigiant Sudanese boys and then milky white, five-foot seven-inch me. The water overflowed, but no one was willing to get out. They drilled me with questions about the hot tub.

"Where do these bubbles come from?"

"This—*what do you call this?* Jet? Are you sure it's good for my back?"

"How do you keep this water so hot?"

The complexities of the "bathtub," as they called it, overwhelmed them. The diving board was nothing compared to the effervescent hot tub.

Over that summer, I became particularly good friends with one of the boys, James. James was educated and mature beyond his years. The place from which he viewed the world was the complete opposite of mine. Driving home that night after the pool party, everyone else fell asleep in the van with their bellies full and their skin smooth with lotion. James sat in the front seat next to me. On that drive home, James chose to share his story of suffering with me.

He asked me if I really wanted to know what it was like being a five-year-old kid in the middle of a war. I eagerly told him yes.

James began to tell me a clear visual story. "Have you ever seen *Saving Private Ryan*? There's a scene at the beginning where all the soldiers storm the beach, and in surround sound you continuously hear bullets gliding by your ears. Each bullet flashes past so close you can almost feel the impact. Meanwhile, people all around you fall, hit by those same bullets that somehow miss you. That's what it was like; you just run. You run from bush to bush. You try to stay alive, and you try to help everyone around you to stay alive. Bullets flew continuously, without stopping. You just keep running."

James was created to lead people. As he ran, he gathered other kids. He knew that the more kids they kept together, the greater their chance of survival. All in all, they formed a large group of hundreds of kids who walked together for two years, finally finding a place at a refugee camp before being sent to America to experience a completely different kind of freedom.

Relationships with boys like James and his cohorts on Ann Street changed me. Those summer months started something in me that morphed and grew in ever-expanding ways, changing the way I saw myself, others, and the world we all inhabit.

I've shared many stories in this book about ways you can reimagine what to do with your excess. Rethinking your relationship with your excess is one way to see your life and the larger world in a different way. But relationships with people result in even larger, more lasting change. Other people have been the greatest catalysts in my life to change the way I see the world.

My desire to embark on these Enough Experiments didn't come from wanting to own less clutter or to save money. This desire came from having personal interactions and ongoing relationships with people who lived their lives with less than I did—from James and his friends sharing their real-life experience of losing everything while simultaneously inviting me into their community of laughter and joy; to Clarence showing up at my door in the sunshine and in the rain, calling me his friend and giving my daughter a one-of-a-kind nickname; to our friend in Nicaragua who graciously invited us to her home. Friendships and relationships change my perspective. Once I change my perspective, I live differently. When we gain a heart of compassion toward others who have less, we want to give more. Our view of what we need radically shifts.

Let's go beyond reevaluating your stuff. I want to challenge you to reevaluate your relationships. Who do you engage as a personal practice to allow yourself to see the world from a different perspective? Name the last time you spent some time with someone markedly different from you—not as a networking tool, but simply for the purpose of seeing the world through someone else's eyes. Do you have any real friends who do not share your same social or economic status? Have you pushed aside the barriers, carved out the time, and intentionally pursued a genuine friendship with someone you wouldn't otherwise see in your typical daily life?

When we walk side by side with another person, we will live differently. As the creative beings that we are, we naturally seek to find ways to make others' situations better. We especially want those we love to have the best life they can have. Our commitment and passion to solve the injustices that plague our friends will push us to find solutions. Married to that will be a burning desire to share the stories of your new friends with others. Others need to know what you learn from your friends. Your personal choice of voluntary suffering in solidarity with those who have less may result in an increase in influence and desire for others to learn from you and join you in your dream to give more.

This is what happened to Andre and me when we started Gift Card Giver three years ago, and this also happened with many others who matched their excess with a need. As you move forward with your Enough Experiment, you may find a synergistic parallel between the needs of others and your personal excess. The result may be an opportunity to turn that experiment into a longer-term project, a sustainable organization, or perhaps even your calling in life. When we realize the opportunity we have to help others, often a simple experiment can turn into a societal solution.

However, I want to give you a word of caution.

Helping others for personal gain benefits no one. Embarking on an Enough Experiment for the purpose of finding your life's calling is misguided. Pursuing a friendship in order to find a project hurts everyone. Start small. Start with your own heart and mind. Push toward defining enough for your personal life first. Pursue relationships for the pure joy of truly connecting with another human created in the image of God. As you take each step, you may slowly start to see creative solutions that you and your new friends can pursue together.

BILLBOARDS TO BAGS

Did you know that if you lined up every billboard created over the course of one year in America in a straight line, it would reach beyond the distance from New York to Los Angeles? In total those billboards would stretch over 2,700 miles. In the old days, advertisers painted ads on billboards, but today, most are simply vinyl banners tied on with rope. The average billboard stays up for about one month and is replaced when the space is sold to a different advertiser. Some people may read this statistic and lament over yet another way advertising negatively influences our lives. Others will quickly diagnose the environmental impact of this extreme excess as it fills up our landfills when advertisers discard vinyl billboards.

Our team saw this as an opportunity to create jobs and make something unique. We believe that the broken can become beautiful again. So we contacted billboard companies to find out if we could get their excess banners. We had a hunch that billboard companies don't actually want to be hazardous to the environment, so we asked them to contribute their excess vinyl billboard banners to us after they've been taken down from the side of the road. Almost immediately, we received loads of this banner material to *upcycle* into new products.

At the same time, we became increasingly aware of refugees in our neighborhood and in the neighboring communities, many of whom were unemployed and struggled to make ends meet. Without knowing our language, customs, or city, they fended for themselves much like my Sudanese friends did. Without financial help or emotional support, newcomers often have a hard time learning to feel at home here. My longtime friend Josh Blackson simultaneously felt a growing passion to create a solution for this pressing problem. The plans started to come together. We decided to open a small shop where we could employ refugees to create bags made out of discarded billboards. Before we finalized any of the details, a conference approached us and asked if they could purchase five thousand bags. At the time, we didn't even own a sewing machine, but we already had billboard banners, people to do the work, and orders to fill. We knew we had to begin.

One year into the project, our team created and sold over seventeen thousand bags, and today, we're constantly creating new products and learning new skills in the process. Presently, we're creating bags for retail stores, our online store, conferences, churches, and organizations all over the world, all of whom hope to make a difference with their purchases.

These Billboard Bags are a microstory of the opportunity that exists to address needs out of our excess. In traveling to other countries I've seen unique products made from upcycled magazines, newspapers, candy wrappers, juice boxes, and plastic bags. Discovering these innovative product designs and ways to create jobs led me to believe that some of the most innovative products we'll see in the generation to come will originate with people in great desperation. Out of their quest for survival, our society will transform. Out of their desperation, we will be educated. Out of their creations, our habits will change. Out of their ideas, we will be inspired. Out of their excess, we will want to be more like them. Out of their stories of brokenness, we will begin to understand something beautiful.

MORE

Over the past few years, I've met other people who started with an experiment and built organizations around the success of their "enough" premise. None of these people started out wanting to initiate entire projects or organizations around their experiments, but they did find an opportunity to better the lives of others and felt a deep conviction to see these experiments turn into sustainable projects. Their experiments eventually evolved into a personal calling and lasting conviction. These stories are examples of how we can turn our excess into a way of addressing a social need.

Broken to Beautiful

In their book, *Veneer*, Jason Locy and Timothy Willard share the story of Dean Brandt, who owns a wood salvage operation. He makes hardwood flooring out of antique wood that he salvages. It's not engineered to look old; there's actually a story to go along with the products he creates.

"The story of the wood makes it unique, and so you appreciate the scratches and the dents and the imperfections," wrote Jason and Timothy. "Dean calls these blemishes the memory of the wood, beauty marks that contribute to the wood's uniqueness. 'The beauty of imperfection.'"[1]

Brian Preston is a creative guy with the ability to make things with his hands. He isn't just an idea guy; he goes beyond that and physically makes his ideas come to life. He sees "the beauty of imperfection" in the world. One day, Brian started collecting old pallets that he would find on the side of the road. He took them into his woodworking shop, sanded them down, and cleaned them up. Over time those wood pieces became something more when he started making furniture out of the excess of others. Brian thought he would try posting a picture online to see if his furniture would sell. He started with tables for the kitchen, side tables for the living room, and desks for offices. When you see one of these tables, you must stop and appreciate the new creation. He takes what is old, beat up, and bruised and then creates a new thing that can only be described as beautiful. Not only are Brian's creations great pieces of furniture, but they are each made out of what others once considered trash. He turned trash into a conversation piece. He took what was broken and made something beautiful.

We all want to be part of a story that is too good to be true. If pallets to tables wasn't a good enough story already, Brian dreamed of how to make them even more significant. His goal is "to create … organizations around meeting the needs of the forsaken and forgotten by leveraging good solid business practices."[2] This table project gave him the leverage to move forward.

"I have a passion … to stop talking about doing good, and actually start doing good," Brian said.[3] For over a year, he interacted on a consistent basis with a community of homeless friends living in a tent village in suburban Atlanta. Out of building relationships with this community, Brian decided to launch his new venture by employing and mentoring one of these men in how to build furniture. Together, they started a furniture business made from reclaimed wood. Brian started Lamon Luther[4] with the belief that dignity is better than charity because it gives freedom and meets essential needs. Brian is a carpenter, and he wanted to share this skill with another individual, hoping to lift someone out of poverty.

Brian gave his friend without a home what my friend Peter Greer, president of Hope International,[5] would refer to as "a hand up, instead of just a hand out." This is what happens when excess meets need: *a new story begins.*

Moving Forward

Whenever conversations with my friends centers around transportation, one thing always comes up: *bikes.* We all have this dreamy hope of a better, environmentally friendly way of transporting our bodies from one place to the other on a bike. Wouldn't it be great to bike to work every day? We wouldn't have to purchase gas, we would get a good workout without a gym membership, and we'd have time to process the day on the way home. Some of us might even take the next step and purchase a bike. Maybe we'd ride it a few times and realize that it's more difficult than one would think. What if we have a meeting that day on the other side of town? What if it's raining? What if we work up a sweat on the way to work? The "what if" excuses emerge very quickly in this all-too-idealistic aspiration, resulting in the bike moving to a closet, shed, or garage.

Eventually we'll buy the classic six-inch S hook from the nearest hardware store and hang the bike, and our aspirations, upside down from the rafters. Three years later, the bike still hangs in the shed from the same hooks, and we haven't ridden it once. Many people own a bike, but few people actually ride their bikes consistently.

Tim and Becky O'Mara have a good use for those bikes. Tim and Becky moved into Adair Park, an Atlanta neighborhood known for crime and poverty in recent years, but with a rich history in the heart of the city. Beautiful homes with great front porches fill the area, but it's in need of restoration and new, hopeful energy. Tim and Becky brought some of that hope to this neighborhood. They quickly gained influence in the neighborhood by spending lots of time with the future of the neighborhood: *the kids*. The kids had energy, and the neighborhood needed physical restoration.

Then the O'Maras thought about those bikes up on S hooks. So they partnered with 12 Stone Church[6] to hold a bike drive. They simply asked for donations of any bikes sitting around in garages, basements, and sheds, and their organization started a new collaborative initiative for the neighborhood. They call it the Beltline Bike Shop.[7] They collected over a hundred bikes in one week. Then they invited the neighborhood kids to earn a bike of their own through community service, such as lawn care, bike repairs, and dog walks. The kids learned basic business skills, accountability, responsibility, and leadership, and they got a bike at the end of the experience. By creatively liberating the excess bikes sitting in garages all over the city, the Beltline Bike Shop transforms how kids see the world and creates a new opportunity for their future. What else is sitting in our homes and storage areas that could be used for good?

Necklace Keeps Giving

What do you do with all your old keys? You know, the keys from an old apartment, keys from an old lock to the shed, side-door keys, or the key to the closet at your last job that you never returned.

I don't know about you, but I have a drawer at home that contains a ring of random keys, and I have no idea what they open. I'm afraid to get rid of them, though, because of the small chance that they fit that one door or that one lock I'll need to open someday.

Caitlin Crosby is a musician who uses old keys to do something transformative. She started The Giving Keys, an organization that's being passed from person to person, telling a simple story of truth and uplifting generosity. They take leftover keys and stamp them with words such as *hope*, *strength*, *faith*, *fearless*, *love*, *peace*, or *dream*. They craft necklaces using the keys and some leather rope or a simple chain. When you buy or are given this one-of-a-kind necklace, you must give it away at some point to a person who you feel needs the message that's on the key. As these keys started getting passed around Los Angeles, Caitlin met Cera and Rob, who were living on the streets in Hollywood. They were sitting under an umbrella in the rain, holding a sign that read: "Ugly, Hungry

& Homeless." So Caitlin hired them to engrave keys for necklaces and ship out the orders.

From all the orders, Cera and Rob made enough money to stay in a motel for a few months. Rob started taking GED classes. A transitional home accepted Cera into their program while she continued to work for The Giving Keys. Cera also got a job at the San Diego Zoo to save up more money and to work toward her goal, which is to become a massage therapist. Rob took his GED and passed with all A's and has moved onto college classes.

Caitlin's generosity started with keys but is now transforming lives as well. Out of old keys, she is forever changing lives.

More Than a Meal

On September 16, 2011, I sent out a thought through Twitter that said, "Cool concept. 10 friends have dinner monthly. Each put $100 on the table. Dinner conversation: what new project do we give to & why." That little tweet spurred on the most response I have ever had on Twitter. People loved it, and one person ran with it. Before I knew it, Scott Tanksley tested it with some friends and chose to give to a single mom in their community that needed some groceries to make it another month. The idea was simple: host a meal and share resources to meet a local need. He started sharing the idea with others, and next thing you know, there were thirty meals that were planned around the city of Atlanta. Anyone can host a meal, and you can determine what you want to give, but communally you decide what need to help out financially.

Meals With a Mission[8] is an easy way to intervene on behalf of others' needs quickly, respectfully, and effectively. In Scott's words to me, "Choose a meal date and a donation amount per person. Invite others. Give anyone who wishes two minutes to share a cause. Vote and leader gets the entire donation."[9] Meals With a Mission created a simple tool to send out invites and are developing a giving mechanism through the organization. Sometimes community can even instigate a greater understanding of needs and can motivate generosity. This simple idea brings people together, makes needs known, and collaboratively brings solutions to suffering in a local and self-organized way.

Clean Hands

From as early as I can remember, my parents taught me to wash my hands after I went to the bathroom. I take a shower every day, my clothes are always clean, and soap is a given in my home. This, however, is not true for everyone. Derreck Kayongo was born in Uganda, into a family that made clothes and soap. Later, war displaced him from his home, forcing him to live in a refugee camp for an extended period of time, after which he immigrated to the United States for a new life of freedom. Derreck has an electric personality. He is always the best-dressed guy in the room, and he wears a smile that lights up everyone around him. Numerous people told me about Derreck's passion, saying that I had to hear his story.

He loves to tell the story of the first time he ever stayed the night in a hotel. He went into the bathroom and noticed multiple bars of soap. He used a bar and wrapped it up so he could use it again later. When he got back to his room, he found that someone had replaced his soap. Uh-oh. He thought that the hotel managers tracked his soap use somehow, so he went down to talk to the concierge and confess what had happened. He felt sure he would be penalized in some way.

You see, in the refugee camp, Derreck didn't get any soap to stay clean. He felt that using soap in this hotel was a luxury, not a necessity. Cleaning his body was such a treat and made him feel good, but still, he thought he'd done something wrong. The concierge reassured him that he could use as much soap as he wanted, and the cleaners would replace whatever he used the next day without any penalties.

Rather than simply use up all the soap and go on his merry way, a lightbulb went off for Derreck that day. Every day, people leave endless amounts of hotel room soaps either partially used or not used at all. What if he could collect this leftover but perfectly good soap and send it to refugee camps all over the world to clean the hands of the impoverished?

Derreck created Global Soap Project.

Global Soap Project collects discarded soap from hotels, reprocesses it into new bars, and gives that soap to vulnerable populations throughout the world. They work with organizations with existing operations in numerous communities to ensure that the soap is distributed to those in need, with the goal of improving health through improved personal hygiene.

With 4.6 million hotel rooms in the United States, an estimated 2.6 million soap bars are discarded every single day. By partnering with Global Soap Project, hoteliers divert tons of waste from the landfill and bolster environmental sustainability programs. Through this program, hotel managers, housekeepers, and guests become more environmentally conscious and more sensitive to the needs of vulnerable populations.[10] Derreck pioneered a new distribution system to help end many unneeded sicknesses that a bar of soap and consistent hand washing can eradicate.

His pursuit of this task is admirable, so why does he do it?

Derreck said, "Every single day you have the opportunity to do something heroic for another person, to make their life a little bit better than it was before."[11] He turned excess that we don't even notice into a solution, meeting needs that only he could understand. Since its beginning, Global Soap Project has formed partnerships with more than three hundred hotels, including the Hilton Hotels. It took a guy who lived through the suffering to see the opportunity.

Enough Car Washes

When many people think of their excess, they focus first on their homes. They analyze their personal assets, wealth, or simply look at the stuff sitting around their house. But what if you took this concept of enough to a business? How would you operate differently, and how would that allow you to wield influence in your industry? Henry Ford, the founder of Ford Motor Company, was a leading thinker in how business must have a deeper meaning. He said: "A business that makes nothing but money is a poor business."[12]

Jim Dudley owns a few car-wash businesses in the Southeast. These car washes are the economy, five-dollar kind that you drive through quickly with the option of personally vacuuming out your car for free on the other end of the tunnel. Jim always wanted to be a business owner who did something remarkable in his industry. He wanted to be a leader living a great story for his company and his family. He had a simple idea. He decided that he would provide clean water for one day to one person without access to clean water every time a car went through one of his car washes. A one-for-one concept is not a new idea, but for the car-wash industry it was unthinkable. *And he did it.*

Within weeks of launching the campaign, Jim received a call from the International Carwash Association, of which he is a member and active collaborator. One of the executives heard his story and called to see if Jim would be interested in sharing his strategy with the entire industry. Jim chose to live a different story, he chose to give back, and his influence instantly expanded. In partnership with other car-wash businesses, Jim and others decided to launch a test campaign across the city of Atlanta for three months. They called the campaign "Wash Away Thirst."[13] In short: one wash gives one day of water to one thirsty person. They quickly had over eighty car washes participate in the city of

Atlanta, and word spread quickly—car washes from nine states and even Canada joined the campaign. In the first six months of washes, Jim's crazy idea brought clean water to two million people.

These businesses chose to give of their excess to address the basic need of clean water across the world.

What's next? I believe that every person can do something. Some of your personal Enough Experiments will change your life and maybe one other person's life as well. Some of your experiments and ideas will change an entire family. Your small change might significantly impact an entire neighborhood in your city. One group's choice to commit together to give up their excess could alter an entire city.

New groups will form. New communities will emerge. Ideas will germinate. Businesses will be born. Corporations will choose a different path.

When we choose enough, it will result in more for the people who need it.

ENOUGH TALK

As you have read in this chapter, these leaders found a way to keep excess at the forefront of their minds. We found a way that everyone can use to turn the realities of excess in life into a constant, transformative reminder. I would like to challenge you to keep an excess bin in your house.

If you are like me, you have a trash can and a recycling bin. What if you added one more bin to your collection? An excess bin. Keep this bin for anything that you are not actively using anymore and could contribute to the needs of others. This bin may be used for a garage sale for orphans, or it could be given to a thrift store periodically, or maybe these things could contribute to a rehabilitation home. By committing to a place to gather your extra stuff around the house, you will keep what you have learned from this book in front of you on a consistent basis and hopefully challenge how you live regularly.

YOUR ENOUGH EXPERIMENT

All life is an experiment. The more experiments you make the better.

—*Ralph Waldo Emerson*

I have a never-ending conversation with my mother. She always asks how I became a creative individual, and I always tell her that I learned from her. I owe much of my creative spirit to her example. She would tell you that while I was growing up she was a stay-at-home mom, but in truth, that was only one of her jobs. In addition, she basically worked full time at our church. My dad was the pastor, while my mom led all of the initiatives for women and college students.

My mom never thought of herself as a creative individual, but every program she created had a flair that only she knew how to bring. In her unique way, she thought through every detail, from how she communicated about the event, to the ambiance of the space, to the takeaway at the end of the gathering. She created wow experiences. When you create a wow experience it is memorable, and it changes you and anyone who becomes a part of it. A wow experience is a social interaction in which a significant emotional transaction takes place. In these experiences, leaders carefully craft a detailed environment and hope for something special to transpire. A wow experience is personal and honest, touched with a little piece of the designer's heart.

There's a little popsicle stand in Atlanta called King of Pops[1] that quickly became a favorite of our city, and word spread fast. Two years after launching, King of Pops sells thousands of popsicles every day and recently opened seven different stands in three different cities. Steven Carse is the founder of King of Pops, and when I once asked him the difference between his popsicles and everyone else, he said, "We use all natural ingredients and fresh fruits, but the real difference is, we put a little love into every single popsicle we craft."[2]

It's a wow experience every time you try their tasty treats.

Steven is a creative individual, my mom is a creative individual, and I believe that you are a creative individual. I invite you to join me and many of the individuals you've read about in this book in conducting an experiment. I want you to challenge what is enough in your own life. In addition to trying some of the projects in this book, my hope is that you'll turn this particular experiment into something special: *a wow experience that transforms your life*.

Create a new social interaction with the potential for a significant emotional transaction. Craft the details carefully, and hope for something special to transpire. Don't limit yourself. My hope is for you to truly change your perspective so you can see your life in a new way.

The last time you conducted an experiment was probably in a middle-school science class, which may have been recent or many years ago. You might be out of practice, but we want to help you in the process. By willingly choosing an experiment, you give yourself a test with a set of requirements or controlled conditions to determine a new personal truth. We usually conduct experiments because we think we know the outcome, but until we try it, we will never be positive. So before you commit to make drastic, lasting changes in your life, try an experiment to see what it might be like. Try a new way. Commit to a reasonable amount of time to determine if this should continue or if it is unreasonable to live your life within these new conditions.

Start with one experiment, and don't be afraid to fail.

Dr. Malinda Schaefer, an HIV Researcher at Emory University, said that "experiments don't usually fail; they may not give the desired or expected results, but that's not considered failure. Even if you decide to end the experiment early, that's still a result—you are learning something about yourself in the process."[3]

The point of this experiment is to experience a way of life that counters your current paradigm and gives your brain an opportunity to see the world in a new way. The purpose is to change and give yourself the opportunity to choose generosity as a lifestyle. Your experiment seats you in a different chair at the table and allows you to see the same conversation from a new vantage point.

There's something stirring within you: you know you have more than enough, and yet you, like me, always want more, desire more, and try to get more. Your wants have increasingly exceeded your needs. You have excess. What is your excess? Write it down:

I HAVE MORE THAN ENOUGH _____ !

What is the most creative and challenging way to change your perspective toward whatever you wrote down? If you cut it out of your life, how would that change your level of strength? What could you do to operate in a radically different way? Imagine a challenge that would be difficult to accomplish but would influence the way that you think forever.

That challenge is your Enough Experiment. Welcome to a new way of living everyday, extraordinary dreams with less than you desire.

Before you move forward too quickly in the details of the experiment, don't forget why you will embark on a quest of personal renewal. Our desire with these experiments is to imagine a new way of living, to imagine how another person lives with less than we do every day. It's important to integrate a new standard of enough into the fabric of our everyday lives because that standard forces us to transition from ignorance to compassion.

Brennan Manning wrote about this in his memoir *All Is Grace*, when he realized the things that he could acquire by gaining more success might not actually be pretty:

> I was roused one morning from a startling dream.
> The dream was essentially that I had achieved all
> my aspirations of status and station. You might

call it "the pretty dream"—pretty wife, pretty
exclusive home, pretty fast car, pretty great money,
and pretty impressive literary awards.... I woke
up in horror to explain, "My God, there's got to
be more!" For a twenty-one-year-old about to set
sail on a course for "pretty," the dream was nothing short of troubling. I thought I'd finally found
some direction and purpose, a path to be me. But
that dream stopped everything in its tracks when I
felt that having it all wouldn't be enough.[4]

When we create a new way, it always forces us to walk paths
others may not have walked before. You choose a new way that has
the potential to become transformational for others. They may not
understand at the beginning, but they will see something different
about the choices you make. Soon, others will ask your advice as
they begin a journey of enough for themselves. You gain influence
by doing something. You do something significant, and you will
become a person of influence in your community.

DREAM

Begin with a Theory

At the start of your Enough Experiment, try to predict your results.
What do you think will happen? Create a hypothesis for the sake

of argument and investigation: this is your unproven assumption.[5] This starting point will create a comparison for your actual end results. We all need a baseline measurement to assess our results (which may be positive or negative). This theory could simply be your assessment of how you feel about your excess. Write down your impressions in a journal, or discuss them with others. Your theory might also be something more tangible like a quantifiable amount of money, physical materials, or even miles walked.

The method you use to assess your baseline theory should be used to assess the end result so an equal measurement can be made. Don't be consumed by your theories throughout the experiment, but consistently evaluate your progress. Whether your theory is later proven or disproven is not the point; I hope the end result will lead you to a value by which you can live in the future. Determining an ultimate value has the ability to define a new way of living.[6]

Questions

What is your starting theory, hypothesis, or premise?

Why did you choose this experiment?

How do you think your life will be different because of this experiment?

After finishing this experiment, what do you hope will be a new value you live by?

What is the end result you are hoping for?

CHOOSE A PERSON IN SOLIDARITY

When I started writing this book, I shared how I believe that out of our excess we can address issues of need and suffering. By choosing to embark on an Enough Experiment, you voluntarily offer your life in solidarity with others. Solidarity means "to suffer with" someone. When you voluntarily choose an act of suffering as your Enough Experiment, it will increase your stakes in the experiment overall. Your lack of excess throughout the experiment will seem meaningless when compared to the reality others live through daily. Have you ever voluntarily chosen to suffer with others? I can promise you that making this choice will add depth to your character and experience.

Here are a few examples of others living in solidarity with a hurting community.

Chris Seay, a pastor in Houston,[7] chose to do an experiment for forty days in which he ate the same food at every meal as the child he sponsors through Compassion International. Chris Heuertz is a codirector of Word Made Flesh,[8] which is based in Omaha, Nebraska, and he voluntarily wears shorts and flip-flops everywhere he goes as an act of solidarity with the street kids that their organization interacts with all across the world. The kids wear shorts and flips-flops, so Chris wears shorts and flip-flops, even on the cold and snowy days in the frigid Omaha winters. You read earlier that my wife, Andre, made a conscious choice to walk to work and back home for forty days. Andre is a physician assistant and serves many impoverished patients living in low-income communities around the city of Atlanta. She chose to walk to work in solidarity with her patients, to know what it feels like to walk through the doors of her clinic sweating, out of breath, and tired. Chris Seay, Chris Heuertz, and Andre each chose to voluntarily suffer with friends as a sign of solidarity.

You may not know another person with a relatable need or concern. Here are a few responses you may have to this portion of the process, along with potential outcomes, as you prepare your experiment or act of solidarity:

1. You know a person with whom you will choose to walk in solidarity throughout the Enough Experiment. *How will you keep that person in constant thought throughout your journey?*

2. You know of a people group that is suffering an injustice in the world today, and you would like to walk in solidarity with them through your Enough Experiment. *How will you share this injustice with others to raise awareness of the problem?*

3. You can't think of a person or injustice that relates to your personal issue of excess. The person or issue with which you want to suffer may not relate to your Enough Experiment. That's okay. You can still choose a person or specific injustice to highlight during your experiment. The act of thinking, praying, relating to, and suffering alongside a person or problem in our

world will only deepen your compassion. *How will you relate your solidarity with that person or problem to your Enough Experiment? How will you keep the injustice at the forefront of your mind throughout the experiment?*

DEFINE CLEAR BOUNDARIES

The next important phase in preparation for your Enough Experiment is to determine the parameters or rules. These are the dos and don'ts, so you know your personal boundaries once inside the experiment. I love how soccer is played in this way. There are clear boundaries for the game to be played, and the ball must always stay inside of those chalked lines, but the players can freely run, play, and explore the game from outside the line and not be penalized.[9]

As much as this experiment is meant for you to practice suffering alongside others, it is also meant for you to enjoy within the boundaries you set up for yourself. It should help you explore a new way of living. So create clear boundaries for the experiment. This is not meant to put you in a box; rather it gives you a place to explore. If the rules are too complicated you will probably be unable to see the experiment through. Fewer boundaries will create a much stronger result, so choose five or fewer boundaries that you can easily share with others. Lastly, determine your experiment's start and end date.

Questions

What are my Enough Experiment boundaries?

1.

2.

3.

4.

5.

Are the boundaries too easy? What would make them more difficult?

How should I simplify these boundaries to clearly communicate to my peers?

When is the start and end to my Enough Experiment?

GIVE EXCESSIVELY

The only gift is a portion of thyself.

—*Ralph Waldo Emerson, "Gifts"*

I've said it many times before: when we choose to live with less, we gain the opportunity to give away more. When you choose to sacrifice a portion of what you have, the result may be the greatest gift you've ever contributed.

The question then becomes, to whom will you give your excess? This is where you will find great joy in the experiment. As you prepare for your journey, determine who will benefit from your sacrifice. Most likely, there will be two forms of excess that will result from your Enough Experiment.

The first kind is the excess that you will just choose not to use during the experiment while you live in solidarity with someone else in need. My one request: don't simply reallocate your excess, lending to another area of your life. Instead, consider giving that excess, whether it's money, time, clothing, or something else, to a person, need, or cause that can use it.

Second, there is the excess that you discover but didn't realize you had throughout the experiment. Share this excess with others when the experiment is complete, if you feel compelled. Giving out of a selfless act of courage is like a little tick forward in the restoration of humanity. Let me take the chance now to affirm you and thank you for your contribution.

Questions

What will I have in excess because of my Enough Experiment?
How and to whom will I give my excess throughout my experiment?
When will I give away this excess?

INVITE FRIENDS

Determining what is enough in life is a very difficult task to tackle on your own. Mike Metzger defined community as "working together."[10] So while it may be a personal decision, the process works best when you work it out with others. You have already made a series of great decisions in preparation for your Enough Experiment; now you have the opportunity to engage your friends to join you. A friend can join you and complete the same experiment that you've already designed. Or a friend can create their own experiment and work out their "enough" journey for themselves while processing with you along the way. Finally, a friend can simply encourage you, process with you, and celebrate with you during and after your Enough Experiment. Any and all options are good. It is your responsibility to invite others into the process. The more you share with others, the more deeply the lessons you learn will become part of your future.

Here's a tip: to be sure that you bring others into the process, create an event for the completion of the experiment before you begin. Set a date, make up an invitation, and send it to all your friends. This will also create accountability to help you see your experiment through to completion. It will also create a support system for when you reach your benchmarks, as well as for when you feel you might be in over your head.

Questions

Who in your life would you most like to invite into this experiment with you, and why?

How will you approach your friend in a winsome way to invite him or her to join you in this experiment?

Who should you tell about your experiment? Who will encourage you along the way, and what are specific ways they can help?

How will you communicate your progress to your friends through-out the experiment?

DO

Begin with a Bang

When you start your Enough Experiment, your emotions, excite-ment, and energy will be high. Feel free to begin big, but be careful of the distractions that might keep you from following through. Regardless of your passion at the start, along the way, you will prob-ably experience a dramatic shock to your system that will tempt you to not complete your experiment.

Here are three common distractions that cause incomplete Enough Experiments:

1. Different Ideas

When the experiment gets difficult, you might be tempted to shift to a different experiment altogether. Scott Belsky talked about this in his book, *Making Ideas Happen*. He called the place where one idea gets hard and the energy for the project drops the Project Plateau. Belsky said, "The easiest and most seductive escape from the project plateau is the most dangerous one: a new idea. New ideas offer a quick return to the high energy and commitment zone, but they also cause us to lose focus. As the new star rises, our execution efforts for the original idea start to fall off. The end result? A plateau filled with the skeletons of abandoned ideas."[11] When it gets hard, we need to cross the plateau and limit our distractions. If we cross the plateau, we're certain to reach new heights.

2. Personal Fears

Every person who has ever done anything significant has always faced doubts along the way. We all must overcome our fears in order to do what we know we ought to do. Steven Pressfield talked about our fear in terms of the "Resistance" within ourselves, which keeps us from pursuing the greatest good. Pressfield said, "Fear doesn't go away. The warrior and the artist live by the same code of necessity, which dictates that the battle must be fought anew every day.... This second, we can turn the tables on Resistance. This second, we can sit down and do our work."[12] We cannot let our fears keep us from pressing on.

3. Justification of Excess

As you begin your experiment, there is a phrase that will creep into your mind: "Your excess is not as excessive as ..." This evil statement is moving your remarkable experience into a comparison and ranking game instead of keeping the focus on solidarity with people who have much less. Make sure that when you critique your experiment, you keep your focus where it started. You will be tempted to compare your excess with those who have more than you, but you're trying to change your thinking to suffer with the poor. This distraction is natural but is a distorted view of truth, and it will ultimately take you away from an experience that will shape new thinking. It's easy to justify our normal way of life, but we are not seeking justification; we are seeking a new way of living.

Questions

What other ideas might distract you from finishing your Enough Experiment?

Write these new ideas down so you can pursue them after this experiment is complete.

What is the greatest fear you have at the beginning of this experiment? How will you overcome this fear?

With whom do you naturally compare yourself, and why?

TRACK YOUR PROGRESS

Every person writes things down in different ways. You may record your findings in a journal, in a blog post, through a tweet, in an email, in a video message, on sticky notes, or with a sharpie on your wall. The format is not significant, but capturing your internal thoughts so you can remember what you are learning is important. Ask yourself, "What am I learning today from my Enough Experiment?" Hopefully, your answer will continue to change and progress over the course of the experiment. This is a great question for your friends to ask you along the journey. When you get to share your experience with others there is an incredible opportunity for world-changing conversations.

Jim Doggett is a cultural architect in the identity movement and founder of The Avalaunch Group,[13] where he works with individuals and organizations on a series of assessment tools to help them find their personal callings and to identify overall potential. I have had numerous conversations with Jim that sparked change. His philosophy? "The only way to change the world is to change the conversation."

We don't control everything happening around us, but we do have control of what we share in conversation with others, right here and right now. Jim also frequently says, "To change the world, we must change our country. To change our country, we must change our city. To change our city, we must change our community. To change our community, we must change the room. To change the room, we must change the table. To change the table, we must change the conversation. The greatest way to change the world is to change the conversation. The more world-changing conversations we have, the greater chance for the world to change."[14] Jim's philosophy has turned into a mantra with young leaders he mentors across the nation. He and one of his significant clients, Boosterthon, started printing stickers with the letters "CTW" (short for Change The World) that they freely give to others. Whenever Jim engages in a world-changing conversation with someone, he asks everyone at the table to sign his or her name on the sticker, and then he places it under the tabletop. It's a street campaign for change. If you ever meet up with Jim for coffee, notice that the first thing he does before he engages in conversation is to look under the table. He dreams of going to a place for the first time, looking under the table, and seeing that world-changing ideas have already interrupted the ethos of the table at which he's seated.

Questions

What am I learning today from my Enough Experiment?
Who should I share my new thoughts with to create intentional conversation?

RESEARCH THE MORE OR LESS

Take time to learn more about your personal struggle of enough. There is always a deeper story that influences why you want, demand, or desire more of whatever it is. Perhaps the history of the product you're focusing on will give you a glimpse into why it matters in your life today. Research the history and how it was marketed to meet a need of consumers. Also, find out who might need this particular product. Make a game of knowing this product better than the person selling it to you does. If you own the story, if you know the tactics and the marketing gimmicks of the seller, you can adopt a more educated response and perspective. Try to discover who makes the product, and then find out who benefits when you buy it. Learn about their living conditions and any other positive and negative aspects of your purchase.

Know everything you can about that thing that you have in excess and the people who need it more than you. Finally, set aside a time of self-reflection to determine why it consumes you.

Tips for Research

1. Find out the big-picture story and history of the product. Why was it originally created, and by whom? What problem did it hope to solve?

2. Develop a series of questions you hope to answer about the items targeted in your experiment, then find the answers or people who can answer those questions for you.

3. As you search for answers, take note of interesting facts, ideas, and findings that stir your curiosity; then feel free to learn more.

4. Don't be afraid to ask someone a question. You will be amazed at what you will find in research through

the power of "the ask." If you find a phone number, make a call. You will always get further and faster when researching information when you talk to a person.

5. Social media is powerful. So if you can't find enough information in your research, ask your question to your circle of friends through social media platforms—you will be amazed by the communal response.

CELEBRATE BIG

You have completed your personal Enough Experiment, so let me be the first person to congratulate you on your accomplishment. You have gained my respect and admiration. You are the type of person who others want to become. You created a discipline for yourself, set a goal, and achieved it. You challenged the status quo in your life, recognized your own excess, and did something significant. Out of your excess you were able to help others in great need. You also chose to journey in solidarity with people who have not experienced the same privilege we've been given.

Often creative individuals are not good finishers, but you actually finished what you started. Often self-proclaimed social innovators wanting to make a difference in the world are great at starting a project but bad at finishing one. *You did both*. I have a feeling that completing your experiment was not easy.

Our team created an exciting but simple way to complete tasks that stretches our attention spans and acts as a great incentive to finish. We celebrate big! What does this mean? When there's a lull in the project, when the details seem greater than the end result, when you are just plain tired, when all excitement and passion has left the building, and when you feel like giving up—that's when we stop everything and dream about how we will end. How will we celebrate? What is the big finale?

Your initial response will be to immediately consume whatever you refrained from throughout your experiment, but I do not recommend that. Be cautious not to have your celebration revolve fully around this thing, whatever it is. You've just completed an epic experiment; don't throw it out altogether without adequate reflection on your reformation. Plus, if you shock your system too quickly, it may backfire.

A friend of mine experienced a negative celebration after a positive journey. This story does not require any names. So I will just call this story "Exhibit A: How Not to Celebrate."

My friend chose to fast for forty days, limiting his food intake to only soups, water, and juices so he could focus on praying through a major decision in his life. When he finished the fast, he decided to celebrate with a dinner at Chili's. He loved their famous baby-back ribs. It sounded like the perfect celebration, but his body wasn't ready for the large amount of food. While he and his wife drove home after dinner, it began. His stomach started growling. He needed to go to the bathroom fast. Something was not right. I'll spare you the details, but let's just say it wasn't pretty.

Sometimes our celebrations may sound great in our minds but are not fitting for our bodies. Choose a celebration that is an appropriate invitation back into your life. Choose a celebration that somehow brings dignity to the person that you walked in solidarity with for the past days. Choose a celebration that will inspire you to complete your task when you want to give up. Celebrate big, celebrate well, and celebrate in an appropriate way.

Questions

How will you celebrate the completion of your Enough Experiment?
In what way will you celebrate your friend in solidarity?
What would be an inappropriate way to shock your system in celebration?
Who do you need to invite to your celebration to join you in the completion?

TELL

Write Your Story of Enough

The easiest thing to do at this point in your journey is to move on. The hardest thing to do now is to reflect on your experiment.

Choose a day to stop and reflect on what you've done. Go to a special place; take paper and a pen and nothing else. Leave your phone, your computer, and any other technology at home or at the office. Start by writing down why, what, and how you did the experiment. Consider the big picture of what you learned from your time of refraining from excess. Consider the questions below as a guide for your reflection. Remember that your story cannot be replicated—only you have lived out this experiment, and your story needs to be captured and shared with others. Reflect on how this dedicated time in your life will impact the rest of your life.

Questions

What are the major differences between your original theory and your findings?

Write down the big picture of the experience: why, what, and how.

Write out the turning points (moments that caused a change of thought) in your journey of enough.

How will you live differently after completing your Enough Experiment?

If you did your experiment again, what would you do differently?

Through your act of solidarity, what will you remember the most?

What conversations did you have with others about your experiment that you will never forget? Why?

What new values have you found that will determine your new way of living?

SHARE YOUR RESULTS WITH YOUR COMMUNITY

You completed your Enough Experiment and captured the story in some way. Now it's your responsibility to help educate others about your findings. Remember, if anyone asks about your Enough Experiment, you should be thankful and feel validated—they genuinely affirm your commitment—but you should never demand that others take the same journey you did. If we judge our friends harshly, we will lose the opportunity to influence them when they truly need our voices in their lives.

Three different types of people will engage you in conversation when your Enough Experiment ends. Be prepared to share with all of them. Don't be offended or surprised by any conversations you have about the experiment, no matter the length. Prepare yourself for each of the types of people who will engage you:

1. The One-Minute Minded—This will be the most common response from your community. They will start the conversation with you by saying something such as, "How did that thing go that you were doing—wait, are you done yet?" They are looking for a short response. "What is the gist of what you did, and how did it turn out?" Have a quick response that communicates what you learned, but not in detail. They don't want the details—just the facts.

2. The Five-Minute Conversationalist—These friends want to learn from your experience. Based on how you respond to the first couple of questions they ask, it could turn into a thirty-minute conversation, or it could simply come to an end. It is best to share the big picture of your project: the why, what, and how. Based on how you respond, they might begin to dig into things you say that strike a cord with their lives in some way. Share honestly and graciously without expectation about where the conversation will go. You should always hope to share about your deep transformation and about what you learned in the process. If you can share these things with your friend, perhaps you can start them on the road to new thinking. Don't be surprised if they bring up your experience again down the road; they will think about it, and you won't even realize it.

3. The Sit-Down-for-a-Meal Learner—These are those friends who want to know everything. They will give you the opportunity to share in as much depth as you want to share. These friends want to know your feelings and thoughts throughout the experience. They want to know the values that you learned and how those values will change the way you operate in the future. Share as much as you desire. Think through how to relate your experience to their lives free of statements of judgment. Think through the questions that

inspired you to perform your Enough Experiment. Ask these great friends if they've ever wrestled through similar questions and how they found resolve. Explore this conversation to its fullness; these friends are usually the people who matter most in your life, and their questions should tell you that you matter to them.

ENOUGH TALK

Now that you have completed your Enough Experiment, we want to hear about it and share it with others so they can gain from the lesson you learned. Write your story, in five hundred words or less, and upload a relevant picture to our website. Please share your story with us so others will be inspired to do their own Enough Experiment. Share your story at: www.moreorlessbook.com/#story.

DRAW YOUR LINE

I have been impressed with the urgency of
doing. Knowing is not enough; we must apply.
Being willing is not enough; we must do.

—*Leonardo da Vinci*

One of my best friends came to my wife with an idea. He wanted to transform our backyard into a community garden. Our property is a quarter of an acre, an unusual plot of land for living in the heart of a major metropolitan city. On a daily basis, the yard is ruled by our dog, Maximus, one of the largest boxers I have ever met; he weighs in at a good seventy-five pounds—part muscle, part curiosity. Andre and Josh instigated a plan to engage me in how to move forward with the community garden. The truth is I really didn't have an option. They wanted a garden, so the question was, when is the tractor going to show up to plow?

The garden challenged me. I started realizing that I viewed my house and my yard as mine. I own it (though technically it will be mine in about twenty-five years when I finally pay the bank for it). This space was mine, and the plans for the garden meant something would happen to my yard that was out of my control. It was all about me. Well, okay, I guess it was Andre and me. This is the second home we've purchased since getting married. We wanted a bigger house and a bigger yard, so we sold our first house and upgraded. It's nothing special to most people. The place is a fifteen-hundred-square-foot, one-story craftsman home that someone renovated a few years before we bought it.

We have more than we need, and it's our responsibility to use this space wisely. We always imagined our home to be a place to host others, with an open door to the community. If you ask our friends they all have access, own keys, and know the code for our security system. We have hosted more than ten different people in our home from anywhere between a month and a year in our extra room. We see our home as a gift to freely share with others. For some reason, I maintained a sense of control with all of the friends who walk through our door.

The garden, however, was the first scenario that felt outside of my control.

Word began to spread throughout our community that the community garden was happening. The next thing I know, twelve people had committed to participating. Everyone agreed to give fifty dollars to fund and start the garden. This money helped purchase supplies, build the fence, and provide seeds, shovels, and fertilizer, and we each committed to tend the garden for one hour each week.

They put the plan in motion, and apparently I was in with or without my consent.

On a Tuesday morning a very loud noise woke me rudely. At 6:30 a.m. a tractor drove into my backyard! *A tractor in the city.*

Before I could put on my shoes and get outside, the tiller started tearing up the grass in my yard. Moments later, an area sixty feet long by forty feet wide, literally one-third of our entire backyard, was dirt. Done. The garden had begun. I stood on our back porch, coffee in my hand, looking at a communal creation I'd never imagined in my own yard. My face changed from shock to a small smirk as Josh looked at me and laughed.

This was my welcome to the garden.

For the next phase we built a fence to keep our dog out of the vegetables. The fence consisted of wood slats three feet high, and chicken wire on the inside with a ledge across the top. Josh PH tested the dirt to assess the quality. Soon after, manure and lime showed up, and we dumped bags of it into the soil. At this moment I accepted the reality that my land was not my own. Then we all dug in, so to speak.

Later, we added a makeshift irrigation system through a series of hoses and sprinklers we picked up from the hardware store for one dollar each. We plotted the land and started spreading seeds for corn, okra, cucumbers, squash, black-eyed peas, snap peas, and more. We put in thirty different shapes and forms of tomato plants and eight green-pepper plants. We now had a farm in our backyard, which is a stretch for me. I'm a meat-and-potatoes kind of guy. Vegetables are the last choice on my list.

We installed a lockbox on the side of the house, so our new garden community had access to keys to our back gate and shed.

About six weeks later everyone celebrated when we picked our first tomato.

That summer, I learned so much about the value of a community working together to do something bigger than any one of us. The truth is that none of us could have accomplished this on our own—the project happened with a unified vision and strong work ethic. Some of the great moments surprised us, and on random evenings I would open our back door and be surprised to find four people covered in dirt and digging up weeds. That summer, we came back from vacation to find a garden overflowing with vegetables. That never would have been possible in 100-degree Atlanta summer weather without others working while we were absent. Some of the best conversations I had that entire year happened while I tended the garden with others. I learned through the garden that the process of losing myself created a much more valuable life and more inclusive community. I was better off because of the contribution of others.

Later that summer, we decided to celebrate our crop together. Family style. Everyone took something from the garden and made a dish to share. I remember sitting around our kitchen table as each person's face beamed with excitement. It was a meal in which we'd all invested. We didn't just buy this food. We had dreamed it, worked for it, and harvested it with our own hands. On the table that night was a variety of tasty treats. We had stuffed green peppers, corn on the cob, zucchini bread, tomato-basil pizza, homemade salsa, fried okra, fresh-picked carrots, fried green tomatoes, and vegetable pasta. We prayed and gave thanks for the meal.

Honestly, and speaking on behalf of our community, I don't think any of us had ever been more thankful for a meal, because we knew God convened with us to provide it. To be clear, I'm still a meat-and-potatoes guy—but that meal was the best I've ever tasted. Somehow it was more than a meal—it was love served on a plate and shared by hands that collaboratively understood creation in a deeper way than ever before.

Just when I think I have a handle on what is enough in my life, I am confronted by new ways to ask the question. There's a continuous line that we all must define and redefine at many different points in our lives. Do we need more, or would we be better off with less? It's not as easy as saying we can live with less in every area of our lives. As we have unpacked in this book, more at times is better, and less can create more opportunities for others.

I believe the purest way to engage the question of more or less is in community. When we open up the conversation and allow others to make decisions with us, the results are greater than something we can come up with on our own. This process of gathering feedback through community is not easy, but the results are good. When you make large purchases, have a conversation with a friend about whether you need it, or whether you just want it. When you choose to volunteer on a project, share what you're doing with others to make sure the opportunity lines up with your passions and strengths. When you evaluate how you live and what is enough, invite the people closest to you to work it out with you. We all have different stories that can make each other's future story better. The more we integrate the question of enough into the ethos of our communities, the greater our communities will become.

One way to change how we approach these questions is simply to share more. Our parents try to teach us to share at a young age, but it's a childlike value that we need to relearn as adults. Instead of viewing your stuff as "mine," view what is yours as "ours." Or take it a step further: "what's mine is yours."

"Every day people are using Collaborative Consumption— traditional sharing, bartering, lending, trading, renting, gifting, and swapping, redefined through technology and peer communities," wrote Rachel Botsman in her book, *What's Mine Is Yours*. "Collaborative Consumption is enabling people to realize the enormous benefits of access to products and services over ownership and at the same time save money, space, and time; make new friends; and become active citizens."[1] Botsman so clearly painted a picture of a new economy where *we* is greater than *I*. Through the garden I learned this lesson well. From borrowing neighbors' tools and equipment, to lessening the burden of weeding by collectively contributing to the task at hand, the garden became not mine but ours.

EXCESSIVE GENEROSITY

Through a life open to community, we learn the needs of others, we are given an opportunity to give to others, and we experience generosity from others. The act of generosity means that we choose to liberally share with others without any personal gain. If you build a life that is separate from people who experience great need, you will always struggle to be a generous person. In large part, the people closest to us determine what we desire. So surround yourself with people who are in need, and you will desire to meet needs. Surround yourself with people living in excess, and your desires will become even more excessive. Generous people live in community with people who benefit from their generosity, which makes for a fuller life for the giver.

Who do you know that is generous? We all have a person we can instantly think of in our lives who embodies the virtue of generosity. My hope is that reading these stories has inspired you to choose a lifestyle of excessive generosity. When I think about people who have been generous to me, there are a few consistent traits that these people embody.

Generous People Have Possessions They Own but Rarely View Them as Only Theirs to Own.

I remember golfing with a guy named Joe. He told me to try out his new driver. I hit the best shot of the day from all the guys playing together. We walked back to our golf cart, and he put the club in my bag. The driver was worth three hundred dollars, and he told me it was meant for me even though he had bought it the week before. It didn't matter to him because his stuff could at any time be more fitting for another person. If there is a need, and he can help with it, he will do it. Generous people view their possessions as temporary; they are joining in a bigger story. Generous people are always looking toward the needs of others by using what they have been given. Things don't matter; people do. They open their house to others. They open their pool for parties. They let people borrow their cars. They freely give, with no returns expected.

Generous People Never Speak about Their Generosity, but Others Do.

My first Apple computer was given to me by a friend named Reggie. We were in a creative meeting, and I was taking notes on a computer that was about four years old. He looked at me and looked at the computer. He folded his laptop and handed it to me and said, "I think you need this more than I do." He had a couple other computers at home. I didn't know what to do. He would not take it back. He handed it to me and never said another word about it. I have told numerous people about how I received that gift from him. Reggie is extremely generous with his time and his possessions. When he reads this, he will probably be embarrassed because he would never want others to know; he just does it. Generous people see what is needed, and they meet the need. We the receivers affirm their generosity and tell others about it because it is rare to meet generous people. We all know generosity when we see it; it is memorable, and we desire to tell others. Generosity is remarkable, and that is why we talk about it.

Generous People Always Give More.

I was on a walk with a friend named Chris. Chris and his wife are missionaries and educators who raise all of their salary from supporters giving to them monthly. One day I talked with him about generosity and what is a healthy amount of money to give to others from what you have been given. He shared with me how their family gives 40 percent of their income to others. I was blown away by his generosity and by how he lives simply. He shared this with me in a very humble way, not to brag, but out of conviction. Generous people never feel like they are giving enough. They want to give more. There is a consistent question that is always stirring in their minds: what am I not being generous with? When we experience the joy of generosity, we always want to give more—this is a healthy addiction and quality. Generous people will consistently choose less to give more.

Generous People Are Thankful People.

My wife and I had dinner with friends named Chris and Lindie. They give to others all the time. Before the dinner, I told the waitress that I was paying for dinner. So when the bill came she gave it directly to me. Chris did not know what to do. He has never had another person pay for his dinner. He always pays. Since that dinner, Chris has mentioned it numerous times. He was thankful and he loves to give, so when someone gave to him it meant that someone truly was showing love to him. Often, generous people don't know how to receive generosity from others, but they are endlessly thankful to be given your gift. They often value thankfulness more than generosity. They give without caring if they are thanked, but when they are thanked their generosity is confirmed. So the word *thanks* is part of how they view the great story they are contributing. Thankfulness is the completion of generosity; it completes a communal experience and giving circle.

THE REDS HAT

It happened on July 23, 2010. Andre turned thirty, and we celebrated at a house we rented on a lake in North Georgia with many of the friends who worked the garden with us. We received a call from a friend in the neighborhood. Clarence had been pushing a lawn mower across the street, looking for work, when he was hit by a car and died. The driver took off. Textbook hit-and-run accident. My friend Clarence was doing the thing that he did every day: he was "looking for work" to survive, and he died along the way.[2]

About six months earlier, Clarence shared with me that he needed some space to store some of his things. He knew that we owned two black rolling trash bins that we often used to haul leaves, weeds, or dirt to our compost pile. Most of the time they just sat empty in our driveway alongside our house. He asked me if he could use those two bins for his few belongings and extra clothes and a blanket to keep safe and dry. We rarely use these bins, and he really needed a place to store his stuff. So I said yes. No questions asked. The bins were his.

After Clarence passed away, I took an hour to clean out those bins and see what he chose to keep. It was mostly clothes. He had a few tools that he had gathered to do yard work for neighbors. There was a DVD player still in the box—kind of random, but I'm sure he thought he could sell it at some point. Looking through the bins gave me time to reflect on his life and think about how important he was to me. Clarence caused me to live differently. He challenged my standards of living. The values I put on my personal gain changed through my interactions with him.

As I reflected on how he changed my life, I saw it—Clarence's Cincinnati Reds baseball cap. It was muddy and faded and the brim was bent, but it was a defining item for Clarence. He wore this hat everywhere. I still can picture him walking away from our house with a quick bounce to his step, a swagger that only he could pull off, looking for some work. Everyone in the neighborhood knew *that* hat belonged to "Clarence," or "Pops," which was his nickname around the neighborhood.

We went to his funeral to pay our respects. I was curious to see how many people would be in attendance. I had never before attended a funeral for a person without a home. More than two hundred people packed the church to celebrate a friend that they knew and loved. We walked in and were handed a program. There was a picture of him wearing his Cincinnati Reds hat on the cover of the program. The service included an open mic time to share stories. For over an hour, friends and neighbors gave testimonies that appropriately honored his personality and charm, his love of others, and the frustrations we all knew that made him uniquely Clarence. It was an open casket, and at the end of the service, everyone walked to the front to see his body for the last time.

As I made my way to the front, I found his mother and handed her the hat we found in his storage bin. We had cleaned it up in preparation for that moment. It was such a defining object that reminded me so clearly of my friend, and I thought she should have it. As I handed it to his mother, her face lit up with clarity and understanding. She recognized the hat immediately.

She shed tears of joy, sorrow, and thankfulness. "Where did you find this? Thank you." There was nothing I could say in that moment. I didn't need to say anything. If you didn't know Clarence, it would mean nothing. But, if you knew Clarence, you knew that hat was the one luxury he cared about. It fit him just right. It was a little style on his head when he couldn't afford a hair cut. I believe that the hat kept his head up when he wanted to give up. He didn't hide in our neighborhood; he was confident of his abilities and shared what he could give to the world.

I didn't have the guts to speak at the open mic that afternoon of the funeral. Since that day, though, I've always wanted to tell Clarence the important role he played in who I am becoming. If I sat with him on my front porch today, I think I would say something like this:

Hey, Clarence. When I read your obituary I found out that your birthday was the same as mine. December 4th. We were born on the same day of the year. So much of your story and mine after that day were miles different both in distance and experience. Yet somehow we ended up living right next to each other. There are so many circumstances that created your story. I have never met a person with a story that has influenced me as much as yours. You frustrated me enough to change how I see the world. Every so often when the doorbell rings, I hope it is you. You taught me that friendships with people different from me create an opportunity for me to be more complete. It is easy for me to be with people who live like I do, and it makes me feel good about myself. When I am with people who live differently, it causes me to change in a good way. You changed my views toward those without homes. You changed what I believe, what I need, and what I want. You changed what I view about what is enough. You inspired this book. I wish everyone had a person in their lives as important as you have been to me. The differences between you and me are significant. On a daily basis I live in excess while you struggled to survive. That contrast forced me to live differently. That is why

I loved you being in my life. I am thankful that
your suffering has come to an end. Thanks for
being my friend. Because of you, I am forced to
live the question: More or Less?

As I reflect on Clarence's life, I still walk in my front door
every day challenged by how much I own. The question is simple.
Even after getting to know Clarence, trying to make a difference,
writing a book, and sharing these stories with others, how different
is my own life?

The question of enough will forever challenge me. I hope it
now challenges you as well. Ask that question of yourself every day.

What is enough?

We face an opportunity every time we ponder the answer.
Many people in the world don't need to answer this question
because they're simply trying to survive. Out of our excess, may
we address the issues of need and suffering all around us. Join me
in creating a new dream, crafting a different story. The only person
who can determine what is enough for you is *you*.

Draw your line today. To live with less, so others can have
more. You have the opportunity to gain a lifestyle of excessive
generosity.

Enough.

APPENDIX

What Is Enough Clothes?

	How many do I have?	How many do I need?
T-shirts		
Tank tops		
Dress shirts		
Casual shirts		
Sweaters		
Sweat shirts		
Jeans		
Dress pants		
Workout pants		
Jackets		
Skirts		
Dresses		
Socks		
Underwear		
Bras		
Dress shoes		
Tennis shoes		
Casual shoes		
TOTAL		

Where can I donate my excess?

When will I clean out my closet?

ACKNOWLEDGMENTS

Thank you.

Bob Goff, you wrote words about me that lifted my spirit and brought me to tears. I hope to have a family like yours and love people how you do. The starting words of this book were inked at the Writers cabin.

Joanna DeWolf, you are more than a big sister to me; you have lived these pages your entire life and sweat over each word with me—thanks for all the time and energy you put into this project.

Gisele Nelson, you make everything I work on better, and again you have outdone yourself with this book. Thanks for believing in me as a leader and friend—a gracious combination.

Dan and Judy Shinabarger, there should be a book written about your generosity; I am living to tell the stories of how you showed me to give excessively to others.

The David C Cook Team: thanks for believing in me and this idea from the first conversation over breakfast. Much thanks to Don Pape, Alex Field, Caitlyn Carlson, Mike Worley, Mike Salisbury, and every other person who has touched the manuscript and brought it to the world.

Christopher Ferebee, you knew this project had legs and saw the potential early on; you made it happen with me.

Nicaragua: this book was written on the streets of Granada at Lily's and Garden Café and was shaped by our relationship with Carmen.

Peter Greer, thanks for asking me for three years to write these stories and share them with others.

Thanks to the people I do life with who have lived this story with me and contributed in unending ways: Josh and Katie Thompson, Russell Shaw, Anne Seymour, Lesley Carter, Kathryn Taylor, Kerry Wilkerson, Brad Lomenick, Jim and Allison Dudley, Greg Gilbert, Brian Preston, Aaron Fortner, Robbie and Mimi Brown, Matt DeWolf, Mike and Karyl Morin, Jon and Beth Gaus, Shayne Wheeler, Dan Adamson, Marisa Wheatley, Josh and Angie Blackson, Kay N'we, Leroy Barber, Charles T. Lee, Mike Foster, Tammy Huizenga, Erin Fisher, Scott Helmbold, Wes O'Callahan, Don and Sandy TenHoeve, Mike and Megin Stearns, Bethany Hoang, Chris Seay, and Ben Washer.

Lastly, I thank Jada Rae and Neko Lee. I hope the two of you someday read these words and make them part of your life. I hope you show me more about generosity than I will ever be able to teach you. You are the future, and I can't wait to see how you do life.

NOTES

CHAPTER 2: ONE MAN'S JUNK

1. MosquitoZapper.com, www.mosquitozapper.com (accessed August 6, 2012).
2. "Tradio: The Bert Show's Crappy Christmas Gift Exchange: What Did We End Up With?", *The Bert Show*, February 16, 2001, http://thebertshow. com/tradio-the-bert-shows-crappy-christmas-gift-exchange-2.
3. Bill McKibben, *Deep Economy* (New York: Times Books, 2007).
4. The Simple Way, www.thesimpleway.org (accessed August 6, 2012).
5. "A Biography of Mayor Rudolph W. Giuliani," April 20, 2005, http://www. nyc.gov/html/records/rwg/html/bio.html.
6. *Random House Webster's Unabridged Dictionary*, s.v. "enough."

CHAPTER 3: THE KITCHEN PANTRY

1. Invisible Children, www.invisiblechildren.com (accessed August 6, 2012).
2. Live Below the Line, www.livebelowtheline.com (accessed August 6, 2012).
3. "New Data Show 1.4 Billion Live on Less than US$1.25 a Day, But Progress Against Poverty Remains Strong," The World Bank, September 16, 2008,

www.worldbank.org/en/news/2008/09/16/new-data-show-14-billion-live-less-us125-day-progress-against-poverty-remains-strong.

4. "Live Below the Line on October 17 – CARE's National Day of Action!" CARE, www.care.org/getinvolved/advocacy/dayofaction/live-below-the-line.asp (accessed August 7, 2012).

5. The Global Rich List, www.globalrichlist.com (site discontinued).

CHAPTER 4: GOOD ENOUGH

1. I first heard this statement from Trent Bushnell, Greater Lansing Youth For Christ.

2. Jon Acuff, *Quitter* (Brentwood, TN: Lampo Press, 2011), 179.

3. Martin Luther King Jr., "The American Dream," in *A Testament of Hope* (New York: HarperCollins, 1991), 210.

4. Google Analytics, www.google.com/analytics (accessed August 8, 2012).

5. Klout, www.klout.com (accessed August 8, 2012).

6. Tom Patterson, *Living the Life You Were Meant to Live* (Nashville: Thomas Nelson, 1998), 27.

7. Steven Pressfield, *The War of Art* (New York: Warner Books, 2002), 165.

8. Mike Foster, *Gracenomics* (Corona, CA: People of the Second Chance, 2010), 63.

9. Eryn Erickson, "Our Story," 2011, http://shop.soworthloving.com/pages/our-story.

10. "Alopecia Areata," WebMD, March 1, 2010, www.webmd.com/skin-problems-and-treatments/guide/hair-loss-alopecia.

11. People of the Second Chance, www.potsc.com (accessed August 8, 2012).

CHAPTER 5: ENOUGH CLOTHING

1. Tara Struyk, "The Only 2 Financial Rules You Need to Live By," Yahoo!
Finance, October 18, 2011, http://finance.yahoo.com/banking-budgeting/
article/113633/only-2-financial-rules-moneytalksnews?mod=bb-budgeting.

2. To learn more about ways that charity can negatively influence the needs of
the poor, I would highly recommend reading *Toxic Charity: How Churches
and Charities Hurt Those They Help* by Bob Lupton, who is the founder
of FCS Urban Ministries and a leader in the community development
movement.

3. Jonathan D. Glater, "Colleges Profit as Banks Market Credit Cards
to Students," *New York Times*, December 31, 2008, www.nytimes.
com/2009/01/01/business/01student.html.

4. Sharon Lechter, "What the New Credit Card Laws Mean for the Next
Generation," Forbes, March 3, 2010, www.forbes.com/2010/03/03/credit-
card-college-students-personal-finance-lechter.html.

5. IWearYourShirt.com, www.iwearyourshirt.com (accessed August 8, 2012).

6. Diana Ransom, "IWearYourShirt Puts a Social Twist on Product Placement,"
Entrepreneur, May 3, 2011, www.entrepreneur.com/article/219562.

7. "Holiday Private Shopping Party," http://shop.nordstrom.com/c/rewards-
private-holiday-shopping-party (accessed August 8, 2012).

8. Mission Year, www.missionyear.org (accessed August 8, 2012).

CHAPTER 6: ENOUGH PRESENTS

1. "Poorest Countries in Central America," Aneki.com, www.aneki.com/poor-
est_central_america.html (accessed August 8, 2012).

2. Andy Stanley, "How to be Rich: Part 1—Congratulations!" (sermon, North
Point Church, 2007).

3. "Generosity," Wikipedia, http://en.wikipedia.org/wiki/Generosity (accessed August 8, 2012).

4. The Advent Conspiracy, www.adventconspiracy.org (accessed August 9, 2012).

5. Gary Chapman, *The 5 Love Languages* (Chicago: Northfield Publishing, 1992).

6. Newsong, www.newsong.net (accessed August 9, 2012).

7. One Day's Wages, www.onedayswages.org (accessed August 9, 2012).

8. Anup Shah, "Poverty Facts and Stats," September 20, 2012, www.globalissues.org/article/26/poverty-facts-and-stats.

9. Eugene Cho, "One Day's Wages," www.catalystspace.com/content/read/article_one_days_wages (accessed August 9, 2012).

10. Eugene Cho, "A Lifestyle of Enough," www.catalystspace.com/content/read/AUG11--a_lifestyle_of_enough (accessed August 9, 2012).

11. *Encyclopaedia Brittanica*, s.v. "social mobility," www.britannica.com/EBchecked/topic/551322/social-mobility (accessed August 9, 2012).

12. Cho, "A Lifestyle of Enough."

13. Cho, "A Lifestyle of Enough."

14. Cindy Simmons, "Wedding Diary #8 OUR WEDDING REGISTRY," Star94 FM, August 29, 2011, www.star94.com/blogs/cindyswedding/blogentry.aspx?blogEntryID=10314934.

15. Wellspring Living, www.wellspringliving.org (accessed August 9, 2012).

16. Simmons, "Wedding Diary #8 OUR WEDDING REGISTRY."

17. "Gifts of Compassion," Compassion, www.compassion.com/catalog.htm (accessed August 9, 2012).

18. "Gift Catalog," World Vision, http://donate.worldvision.org/OA_HTML/xxwv2ibeCCtpSctDspRte.jsp?go=gift&&section=10389&prod=Q1tLDb3vNqtskSr8oyUxZRhd:S&prod_pses=ZG354D13BF34838E6D5067EC71F78AAEA743E7856874844A1E74BE12F7F1EC733CBCA89EADCFFB8A943A9254C61BCA4A5BC90508BD12135A48 (accessed August 9, 2012).

19. Heifer International, www.heifer.org (accessed August 9, 2012).

20. Hope International, www.hopeinternational.org (accessed August 9, 2012).

21. Samaritan's Purse International Relief, www.samaritanspurse.org (accessed August 9, 2012).

22. International Justice Mission, www.ijm.org (accessed August 14, 2012).

CHAPTER 7: ENOUGH TRANSPORTATION

1. "Jean Vanier, Founder of L'Arche," L'Arche, www.larche.org/jean-vanier-founder-of-l-arche.en-gb.23.13.content.htm (accessed August 14, 2012).

2. Jean Vanier, *Community and Growth* (Mahwah, NJ: Paulist Press, 1989), 72.

3. Bob Dylan, "Brownsville Girl," *Knocked Out Loaded* © 1986 Special Rider Music.

4. Dylan, "Brownsville Girl."

5. Lesley Carter, interview with the author. Used with permission.

6. Carter, interview with the author.

7. Carter, interview with the author.

8. Carter, interview with the author.

9. Carter, interview with the author.

10. Rich Morin and Paul Taylor, "Luxury or Necessity? The Public Makes a U-Turn," Pew Research Center, April 23, 2009, www.pewsocialtrends. org/2009/04/23/luxury-or-necessity-the-public-makes-a-u-turn.

11. Joanna DeWolf, interview with the author. Used with permission.

CHAPTER 8: ENOUGH TIME

1. "Cedar Bend," Spring Arbor University, www.arbor.edu/Cedar-Bend/New-Student-Orientation/Student-Development-Learning/Index.aspx (accessed August 14, 2012).

2. "Euchre," Wikipedia, http://en.wikipedia.org/wiki/Euchre (last modified August 7, 2012).

3. Gretchen Rubin, *The Happiness Project* (New York: HarperCollins, 2009), 85.

4. Michael Karnjanaprakorn and Scott Belsky, "Encourage Daylighting," 99U, http://99u.com/tips/5766/encourage-daylighting.

5. Nisha Gupta, "The Saatchi Y-Spot: Slash/Slash," Hudson/Houston, June 11, 2010, www.hudsonhouston.com/2010/06/the-saatchi-y-spot-slashslash.

6. Gisele Nelson, interview with the author. Used with permission.

7. Nelson, interview with the author.

CHAPTER 9: ENOUGH ACCESS

1. "Inside the Actor's Studio," Bravo, www.bravotv.com/inside-the-actors-studio/ (accessed August 14, 2012).

2. Ruth Haley Barton, *Strengthening the Soul of Your Leadership* (Downers Grove, IL: InterVarsity Press, 2008), 182.

3. Daniel J. Boorstin, *The Landmark History of the American People: From Plymouth to the Moon* (Littleton, CO: Sonlight Curriculum, 1987), 134–36.

4. "Super Size Me," International Movie Database, www.imdb.com/title/tt0390521 (accessed August 14, 2012).

5. Brandon Hatmaker, *Barefoot Church* (Grand Rapids: Zondervan, 2011), 22.

6. "Martin Luther King Junior National Historic Site," National Park Service, http://www.nps.gov/malu/index.htm (accessed August 14, 2012).

7. "Essential2Life," http://e2lonline.com (accessed August 14, 2012).

8. "Friday Five // Darrius Snow," Plywood People, September 10, 2010, http://plywoodpeople.com/3835.

9. "Friday Five // Darrius Snow," Plywood People.

10. H. M. Cauley, "Bankhead Teen Wins Nickelodeon Award," *Atlanta Journal-Constitution*, November 27, 2009, www.ajc.com/news/bankhead-teen-wins-nickelodeon-216112.html.

11. Dale Carnegie, *How to Win Friends and Influence People* (New York: Simon & Schuster, 1982), 54.

CHAPTER 10: BLACK & RED

1. Kevin Drum, "Black Friday," *Mother Jones*, November 26, 2010, http://motherjones.com/kevin-drum/2010/11/black-friday.

2. Kevin Drum, "Black Friday."

3. "Color Psychology and Marketing," Precision Intermedia, www.precisionintermedia.com/color.html (accessed August 15, 2012).

4. Tim Sanders, *Today We Are Rich* (Carol Stream, IL: Tyndale, 2011), 6 –7.

5. Steve Eng, "The Story Behind: Red Letter Bible Editions," *Bible Collector's World*, Jan/Mar 1986, www.biblecollectors.org/articles/red_letter_bible.htm.

6. "Doing the most good" is a tagline created by the Salvation Army.

7. HelpOneNow, www.helponenow.org (accessed August 15, 2012).

8. Garage Sale for Orphans, www.garagesale4orphans.org (accessed August 15, 2012).

9. "The Story," www.garagesale4orphans.org/the-story, Garage Sale for Orphans (accessed August 15, 2012).

10. Blake Mycoskie, *Start Something That Matters* (New York: Spiegal & Grau, 2011), 167.

CHAPTER 11: ENOUGH GIFT CARDS

1. Fivestone, www.fivestone.com (accessed August 16, 2012).

2. Susanna Kim, "$41 Billion in Unused Gift Cards Since '05," ABC News, December 29, 2011, http://abcnews.go.com/Business/unused-gift-cards-shrinking/story?id=15249093#.UC0XQUTjmUc.

3. "Gift Card Statistics," Gift Card Granny, http://www.giftcardgranny.com/statistics/ (accessed September 24, 2012).

4. Stephen J. Dubner and Steven D. Levitt, "The Gift-Card Economy," *New York Times*, January 7, 2007, www.nytimes.com/2007/01/07/magazine/07wwln_freak.t.html.

5. Kim, "$41 Billion in Unused Gift Cards Since '05."

6. Christopher Quinn, "Gift Cards Regifted to Help Those in Need," *Atlanta Journal-Constitution*, November 3, 2009, www.ajc.com/news/gift-cards-regifted-to-184556.html.

7. "Gift-Card Charity," CNN, December 20, 2009, www.cnn.com/video/?/video/living/2009/12/20/whitfield.gift.givers.cnn?iref=allsearch.

8. Ann Hynek, "New Year, Recycled Goods, and Free Games," FOXBusiness, December 31, 2009, www.foxbusiness.com/personal-finance/2009/12/31/new-year-recycled-goods-free-games.

9. "Gift Card Giver," World Vision Report, February 14, 2009, www.worldvisionreport.org/Shows/Stories/Week-of-Feb-14-2009/Gift-Card-Giver.

CHAPTER 12: MAKING ENOUGH MORE

1. Timothy Willard and Jason Locy, *Veneer* (Grand Rapids, MI: Zondervan, 2001), 23.

2. Brian Preston, "What's Next for the Preston Family," October 25, 2011, http://brianpreston.tumblr.com/post/11916802502/whats-next-for-the-preston-family.

3. Preston, "What's Next for the Preston Family."

4. Lamon Luther, www.lamonluther.com (accessed August 16, 2012).

5. Hope International, www.hopeinternational.org (accessed August 16, 2012).

6. 12 Stone Church, http://12stone.com (accessed August 16, 2012).

7. Beltline Bike Shop, www.beltlinebikeshop.org (accessed August 16, 2012).

8. Meals with a Mission, www.mealswithamission.org (accessed August 16, 2012).

9. Scott Tanksley, conversation with the author. Used with permission.

10. Global Soap Project, www.globalsoap.org (accessed August 16, 2012).

11. Derreck Kayongo, "A Message from Derreck Kayongo," Global Soap Project, December 13, 2011, www.globalsoap.org/news/a-message-from-derreck-kayongo.

12. Simon Mainwaring, *We First* (New York: Palgrave Macmillan, 2011), 118.

13. WashAwayThirst.org, www.washawaythirst.org (accessed August 17, 2012).

CHAPTER 13: YOUR ENOUGH EXPERIMENT

1. To taste King of Pops for yourself, check out www.kingofpops.net (or visit them on the corner of Highland and North in Atlanta next time you are in town).

2. Steven Carse, "Plywood Presents Making Ideas Happen Interview" (interview at Plywood People event).

3. Dr. Malinda Schaefer, conversation with the author. Used by permission.

4. Brennan Manning, *All Is Grace* (Colorado Springs: David C Cook, 2011), 88.

5. *Merriam Webster Dictionary Collegiate Edition*, s.v. "theory," www.merriam-webster.com/dictionary/theory.

6. Inspired by a quote from Ignazio Silone, *The God that Failed* (New York: Columbia University Press, 2001), 102: "Liberty … is the possibility of doubting, the possibility of making a mistake, the possibility of searching and experimenting, the possibility of saying No to any authority—literary, artistic, philosophic, religious, social, and even political."

7. Ecclesia, www.ecclesiahouston.org (accessed August 17, 2012).

8. Word Made Flesh, www.wordmadeflesh.org (accessed August 17, 2012).

9. TMBbrand, "TMB Panyee PC short film," YouTube, March 13, 2011, www.youtube.com/watch?v=jU4oA3kkAWU.

10. "Dear Artists…" catalystspace, April 29, 2008, www.catalystspace.com/catablog/full/dear_artists.

11. Scott Belsky, *Making Ideas Happen* (New York: Penguin, 2010), 71.

12. Steven Pressfield, *The War of Art* (New York: Black Irish Entertainment LLC, 2002), 14, 22.

13. Avalaunch, http://avalaunchgroup.com (accessed August 17, 2012).

14. Jim Doggett, email to the author. Used with permission.

CHAPTER 14: DRAW YOUR LINE

1. Rachel Botsman and Roo Rogers, *What's Mine Is Yours* (New York: HarperCollins, 2010), xiv.

2. Christian Boone, "Hit-and-Run Driver Kills East Atlanta Man Blocks from Mother's House," *Atlanta Journal-Constitution*, July 26, 2010 (page discontinued).